CLASSROOM
HABITUDES

TEACHING HABITS AND ATTITUDES
FOR 21ST CENTURY LEARNING

ANGELA
MAIERS

· REVISED EDITION ·

Solution Tree | Press

a division of
Solution Tree

555 North Morton Street
Bloomington, IN 47404
800.733.6786 (toll free) / 812.336.7700
FAX: 812.336.7790

email: info@solution-tree.com
solution-tree.com

Visit **go.solution-tree.com/instruction** to download the reproducibles in this book.

Printed in the United States of America

16 15 14 13   3 4 5

Library of Congress Cataloging-in-Publication Data

Maiers, Angela.
  Classroom habitudes : teaching habits and attitudes for 21st century learning / Angela Maiers. -- Rev. ed.
      p. cm.
  Includes bibliographical references and index.
  ISBN 978-1-935542-62-9 (perfect bound : alk. paper) -- ISBN 978-1-935543-60-2 (library edition : alk. paper)
  1. Motivation in education. 2. Classroom environment. 3. Effective teaching. I. Title.
  LB1065.M276 2012
  370.15'4--dc23
                        2012005864

Solution Tree
Jeffrey C. Jones, CEO
Edmund M. Ackerman, President

Solution Tree Press
President: Douglas M. Rife
Publisher: Robert D. Clouse
Vice President of Production: Gretchen Knapp
Managing Production Editor: Caroline Wise
Senior Production Editor: Joan Irwin
Copy Editor: Rachel Rosolina
Proofreader: Michelle Cohen
Text Designer: Jenn Taylor

Cover Designer: Pamela Rude

ACKNOWLEDGMENTS

This section has been the most thrilling part of writing the book. It is a wonderful and important reminder that we are loved and that we do nothing alone.

I have been blessed with a network of friends, family, colleagues, and mentors too large to name here, but whose support and encouragement have been an integral part of my happiness and strength over the past year. I am humbled and excited to know that every word in this book has been shaped by the people in my life. I hope that I have written in a way that honors their genius and their contributions to my learning and life.

I have great respect for and wish to thank the entire team at Solution Tree. You have made the difficult process of publishing a book smooth, powerful, and rewarding. Special thanks to Robb Clouse for your insightfulness, encouragement, and support. I am especially indebted to Diana Brace and to my editor, Joan Irwin, who edited this book assiduously and with great passion for its potential.

Thank you to all the teachers, leaders, and students who have graciously allowed me into their classrooms and trusted me to teach and learn with them. Your lessons have forever changed me.

I am so grateful to my family, who kept the fires burning and reminded me that I still had a home waiting for me as I traveled nonstop, spreading the message of the habitudes' powers to schools and classrooms across the globe. To my children, Abby and Ryan, whose future I thought of with every word I wrote. To my husband, Bob, who for twenty years has supported every book, project, and wild idea I had to change the world. I know you said, "No more books," but I am grateful you did not mean it. You gave me the time, space, and unwavering support to make sure this one got into the hands of educators. You are my life partner in this world changing; for that I am blessed.

And finally, a huge thank you to the readers past and present who take time out of their full schedules and busy lives to consider how these conversations can shape the learning and lives of the students in their presence.

Without you, these are only wild ideas.

With you, lives will change.

Solution Tree Press would like to thank the following reviewers:

Mary Alexander
Mathematics Teacher
Broadway High School
Minneapolis, Minnesota

Nancy Bensfield
Eighth-Grade Mathematics Teacher
Sandburg Middle School
Elmhurst, Illinois

Shari Daniels
Third-Grade Teacher
Challenger Elementary Schools
Thief River Falls, Minnesota

Jennifer Felke
CTE/Business Education Instructor and Staff
  Development Director for the School of Inquiry
Plymouth High School
Plymouth, Indiana

Janet Reece
Spanish Teacher
Glenbard East High School
Lombard, Illinois

Pernille Ripp
Fourth-Grade Teacher
West Middleton Elementary School
Verona, Wisconsin

> Visit **go.solution-tree.com/instruction** to download
> the reproducibles and access live links to websites in this book.

TABLE OF CONTENTS

Reproducible pages are in italics.

ABOUT THE AUTHOR

Angela Maiers is an educator, speaker, consultant, and professional trainer known for her work in literacy, leadership, and global communications. She has spent more than twenty years working in elementary, middle, and university settings as a classroom teacher, reading specialist, coach, special programs facilitator, and university professor.

She uses her passion for literacy, learning, and social media to discover creative ways to assist schools and organizations in meeting their learning and productivity goals. Angela is at the forefront of new literacy and web 2.0 technologies. Deeply committed to helping learners understand the transformational power of technology, Angela has facilitated the integration of web/digital literacy, video conferencing, webinars, and multimedia platforms into a range of schools and organizations. She also works closely with schools to renovate curriculum, cultivate culture and climate reviews, and develop online courses.

Angela earned a master's degree in educational supervision and reading at the University of Iowa.

To learn more about Angela's work, visit her website at www.angelamaiers.com or follow @angelamaiers on Twitter.

To book Angela for professional development, contact pd@solution-tree.com.

Redefining Success in the 21st Century

The only thing that interferes with my learning is my education.
— ALBERT EINSTEIN

Several summers ago, I was asked to work with a school district putting together its framework for 21st century learning. The agenda included conversations about goals for students in global literacy, advanced understandings in technology and media, innovation, creativity, and collaborative problem solving.

As we worked through the robust objectives defined by such organizations as the Partnership for 21st Century Skills (www.p21.org) and the International Society for Technology in Education (www.iste.org), we realized that success in the 21st century requires the ability to:

- See the challenge and the solution from every angle
- Know what questions to ask and when to ask them
- Communicate one's vision passionately and persuasively
- Connect with others and create an enduring relationship
- Understand your strengths and the discipline needed to improve your weaknesses
- Stand out, stand up, and stand beside, knowing when each is required
- Dream, set audacious goals, and believe they can be accomplished
- Lead, serve, and honor others

As we examined these requirements, looks of concern and frustration spread across the faces in the room. One brave teacher spoke up: "Angela, I'm a kindergarten teacher. I'm really worried about the number of kids coming into my classroom who don't even know how to spell their names. How on earth am I going to add teaching these 21st century skills to my plate?"

No teacher or leader in that room or elsewhere questions the importance of 21st century skills and competencies. To the contrary, these educators are advocates and believers in the urgency for schools to do whatever is necessary to prepare students for successful citizenship in the 21st century world and workforce. The participants' frustration stemmed from the lack of practical, real-world advice on how this implementation might look and feel in the classroom, something that few organizations had been able to communicate in a way that makes sense to those doing the day-to-day work with children. For implementation to happen, we need answers to questions like those Cathy, our kindergarten teacher, posed:

- How does it look with kids who are struggling to read or write their first name?

- How does it sound when I am talking to fifth graders?

- When does this implementation take place? During reading? In math class?

- If I take time away from my content to do this stuff, what will happen?

- And the most commonly asked question—Where on earth do we begin?

Being able to answer these critical questions for teachers was the impetus for *Classroom Habitudes* (Maiers, 2008), the first edition of this book. I wanted to dissect the research in a way that would show teachers how to use what they already teach—content knowledge and literacy and math skills—to help students think critically, collaborate with others, solve new problems, and adapt to change across new learning contexts. For *Classroom Habitudes* and this revised edition, I drew upon a number of sources that provided support for adapting instruction to meet the demands of learning in the 21st century (see American Association of School Librarians, 2007; Bellanca & Brandt, 2010; CTB/McGraw-Hill, 2008; North Central Regional Educational Laboratory & the Metiri Group, 2003; Partnership for 21st Century Skills, 2003; Rivero, 2010; Tapscott, 1998).

The Seven Habitudes

Initially, I focused my attention and work around six key areas that emerged as being most critical in fostering the thinking, problem solving, innovation, and creativity skills identified in the research. I called this 21st century skill set the *habitudes*. The traits that constitute the habitudes are both habit and attitude: daily disciplined decisions that successful learners choose to make and a specific attitude that demonstrates a new mindset and way of thinking about the world

and one's place in it. The six habitudes defined in the first edition of this book
included:

1. Imagination

2. Curiosity

3. Self-awareness

4. Courage

5. Adaptability

6. Perseverance

Four years and hundreds of lessons later, I now know that students who possess these habitudes will become passionately fierce learners. They believe they
can solve any problem and that no challenge is too great. Regardless of the context and circumstance, they approach problems with an attitude of optimism,
persistence, confidence, and resolution to improve the situation. Students with
these habitudes can and will change the world. Over time, I have become aware
of another trait that sustains these behaviors. Passion is a powerful attribute that
enhances the ability of individuals to pursue and achieve their goals. I have added
passion as the seventh habitude of the skill set in this revised edition.

The 21st century world needs learners to *be* critical, to *be* creative, and to *be*
strategic. The 21st century world demands citizens *do* their own thinking, rather
than rely on someone else to think for them. The 21st century world expects
leaders to *have* the endurance, fortitude, and courage to brave each new challenge with confidence and competence. These three concepts—to be, to do, and
to have—are central to helping students become lifelong learners. The learning habits and attitudes that we teach our students will enable them to become
effective contributors to this world. From my personal experience, I know that
teaching the habitudes can and does change lives. I believe these seven habitudes
represent essential behaviors for improving your students' performance in school
and in the world beyond. Let's consider the definitions of the habitudes.

The *imagination* habitude is defined as follows:

> Imagination is the ability to create new images out of thoughts, memo-
> ries, and sensory information, and from those images to mold ideals, role
> models, heroes, loves, concepts, perceptions, and ideas on how to thrive
> and survive.

The *curiosity* habitude is defined as follows:

> Curiosity is a mindset and a willingness to explore the internal and exter-
> nal worlds by asking questions, seeking answers, and engaging in a wide
> range of personal and interpersonal activities.

The *self-awareness* habitude is defined as follows:

> Self-awareness is the ability to use a system of checks and balances to understand ourselves and to make conscious choices and deliberate decisions about the direction and quality of our lives.

The *perseverance* habitude is defined as follows:

> Perseverance is the ability to sustain interest, effort, and commitment in any circumstance that life presents.

The *courage* habitude is defined as follows:

> Courage is the ability to enter the unknown by confronting challenges, taking risks, and overcoming fears.

The *passion* habitude is defined as follows:

> Passion is the ability to intentionally pursue actions that are personally and socially meaningful.

The *adaptability* habitude is defined as follows:

> Adaptability is the ability to cope with change, to recognize its positive and negative aspects, and to manage one's actions to address the nature and scope of change.

Teaching these learning habits and attitudes fosters independence in our students. The habitude dispositions enable them to think critically, make informed decisions, share knowledge, and assume responsibilities.

Why the Habitudes Matter to Students and Teachers

These seven habitudes constitute a life focus for today's students whose lives may be affected by circumstances and situations beyond anything we are currently able to predict or envision. From working with teachers and students, I have discovered that teaching the habitudes is far more than a fulfillment of newly adopted curriculum mandates. The habitudes provide the context in which teachers can communicate with conviction that they believe in the students and their ability to do great things, things that can change the world for the better. The habitudes foster a promise that:

- All children will be prepared to make lasting contributions to the society in which they live

- All children are capable of and can achieve greatness

- All children have the skill and wherewithal to lead lives that are intellectually engaged, productive, and meaningful

- All children have a gift ready to be unwrapped and shared with the world

The habitudes enable students to become critical, creative, and strategic learners. With these characteristics, students' ability to think for themselves is enhanced, and they will have experiences that foster endurance, fortitude, and courage—attributes that will sustain them as they advance through school and life.

In considering how students benefit from studying the habitudes, we also need to focus on ways in which the habitudes are integral to our lives as teachers. I often remind teachers: *We must be the learners and leaders we wish our students to be*. It is not unusual for teachers to query me about the habitudes and why they should take time to add this study to their already crowded schedules. The answers to seven frequently asked questions are found throughout this book, but a few summary answers follow:

1. **Are the habitudes lessons supported by research?** The sources in the reference list reveal the range of evidence that supports instruction in the habitudes. I have relied on guidelines from the Partnership for 21st Century Skills (www.p21.org), a national organization that provides resources that support a vision for learning to ensure 21st century readiness for every student. These guidelines are developed in the *Framework for 21st Century Learning* (www.p21.org/overview), which provides the most clear and well-articulated vision for what 21st century learning encompasses.

2. **Which habitude is best to start with?** Once students are familiar with the concept of the habitudes and have consistent language to talk about these habits and learning dispositions, you can begin anywhere. Activities to develop awareness of the habitudes are described in chapter 1. Because habitude study is all about fostering independence in our students, many teachers opt to focus on self-awareness first. However, the order in which you teach the habitudes is up to you. The approach to teaching the habitudes is described in more detail in the sections that follow in this introduction.

3. **How can I teach the habitudes lessons if I have my students for only forty-five minutes?** Each lesson is intended to be a short and natural conversation with the students. The lessons can take place anytime throughout the day. For a more structured schedule on block time, consider allotting ten to fifteen minutes once a week to focus on a specific habitude you wish students to be aware of during their study. The lesson narratives presented in this book are models you can adapt to meet your teaching style and the needs of your students.

4. **How do I balance the habitudes study with the core curriculum?** I hear this every day from teachers. They believe in the need and urgency of teaching these 21st century skills but worry that the instruction takes

time away from the content they are held accountable for. Although I would love to say the habitudes are the core curriculum, I understand the pressure of curriculum and assessment mandates. I urge you not to see habitudes and content as two separate agendas. Both are needed and serve one another in the interests of helping students become successful learners.

5. **What if the students have already heard the lessons?** This problem is exactly what we want. The habitudes framework supports and aims to achieve systemic implementation across every grade level and content area. Over time, you will notice how the students' growing familiarity with the habitudes fosters a growth mindset and contributes to improvements in their performance.

6. **What do I send home to parents when I begin the habitudes study?** Before our classroom activities included discussions around 21st century skills of innovation, creativity, and global collaboration, it was common practice to send our students home with a worksheet of skills to do or share with their families or caregivers. However, the habitudes are not a *to do* list, they are a *to be* list. Many adults may not be familiar with these concepts or may struggle to support the habitudes in conversations at home. I suggest an introductory letter explaining the purpose of the habitudes and describing the ones you will be teaching and how these lessons will help the students. Once the habitudes lessons are underway, you could let students take their habitudes notebooks home to share with their families. (See appendix A, page 129, for the description of the habitudes notebook.) You could also use the habitudes notebooks in conferences to show parents and caregivers examples of their child's work.

7. **Where can I get more lessons?** A collection of technology tools and web resources for additional lessons for each habitude are available at **go.solution-tree.com/instruction**. Here you will be able to click the links straight from the website.

Learning about and applying the habitudes provide students with unique opportunities to become more fully informed about themselves as individuals and members of society. However, occasions may arise in which some students may view the activities and topics as personally intrusive. The special knowledge you have of your students will enable you to adapt the activities to deal with such situations. A classroom environment that fosters a climate of respect is a necessary element in teaching the habitudes. In such an environment, students are engaged, feel that they are being taken seriously, and know that they can take risks without negative consequences (Cohen, Cardillo, & Pickeral, 2011).

How This Book Is Organized

Classroom Habitudes is more than a *how-to* guide for teaching 21st century skills and competencies. It is a *how-to-be* guide that provides a clear and explicit profile of the learner, worker, and citizen the world requires now and in the future.

Classroom Habitudes contains nine chapters; eight define the habitudes and describe activities for teaching them, and one offers some final thoughts about the concepts. Each chapter is organized in service of the *to be* concept and provides guidance for you in modeling, demonstrating, and supporting students' practice as the learners and leaders I know they can become with your guidance. The appendices provide additional resources, directions for creating and using the habitudes notebook, and a tool for assessing students' understanding of the habitudes before and after their study.

The activities, tools, and strategies presented support the challenging work and improved academic understanding in all subject areas. The habitudes represent the encompassing behaviors, dispositions, and thinking required to operate successfully as a learner in all disciplines and subject areas. Consequently, there are no habitude lessons specific to math, fine arts, or any other subject areas.

What's New in This Revised Edition

What more is there to say about the habitudes? I have learned so much from the teachers who have read the first edition or learned of the lessons on my blog. These educators have pushed my thinking, challenged the ideas, and offered invaluable insights that I would never have considered possible. I am awed at the energy, creativity, and intelligence they display as they apply the concepts in their own lives and their work with learners. This book is a reflection of what teachers have taught me and a representation of our collaboration and collective thinking. Working with and beside them has helped me see how capable we all are and how far we can go with just one simple conversation. This profound admiration and gratitude inspired me to take those conversations even further and deeper in this book. I have added six new elements.

1. **More lessons**: I have added more than twenty new lessons to be interspersed with those familiar and favorite conversations. You will still see the familiar favorites along with many additional materials and resources to support your work with students and colleagues.

2. **A new habitude**: *Passion* is a new habitude I have discovered. At first, I struggled with whether passion was an outcome of an individual or an organization having the habitudes, or if indeed it was a habit and mindset that must be practiced and nurtured. I am absolutely convinced the latter is true and that passion deserves singular attention. I

hope that as you engage in passion-driven conversations with me and others, you will soon agree.

3. **More structure**: Teachers have loved the individual habitudes lessons but have asked me for a more comprehensive framework to structure them. In chapter 1, I describe the instructional framework, which consists of three parts: Name It, Claim It, and Sustain It.

    The framework supports the implementation of a single habitude study or a school's efforts in using the habitudes. You will be pleasantly surprised at the ease with which you will be able to implement the framework across grade levels and areas of study.

4. **More support**: Throughout the book you will see this symbol.

    Perhaps you have seen these symbols in advertisements. These symbols are referred to as *QR (quick response) codes* and are powered by Tag Technology. (See http://tag.microsoft.com for an explanation of this technology.) To access the QR code, you download the tag application on any smart phone or tablet. Once you have downloaded the app, you open the application and take a picture of the code using your phone camera. The app redirects the code to a website using your phone's web browser.

    QR codes are electronic gateways to the supplemental material and real-life examples that support the lessons you are reading about in this book. The QR codes link to video lessons, speeches, blogs, interviews, and additional support materials that will help deepen your understanding of the lesson and extend your learning beyond anything the book itself could embody. Consider the QR codes as your personal invitation into classrooms and conversations from across the world. Here you will encounter real teachers, real kids, and real conversations that you can see, hear, and take back into your own classroom.

5. **More reflection**: The habitudes notebook is intended to teach learners to take responsibility for their individual thinking and learning during habitude study. As I considered the idea of the notebook, I thought about Leonardo da Vinci, who carried a notebook with him at all times so he could jot down ideas, impressions, and observations as they occurred. Like da Vinci, students can use their notebooks to record their impressions of the lessons they have explored together. Everything you need for setting up the habitudes notebook can be found in

appendix A (page 129). Your students will have a choice of keeping track of their thoughts and questions in traditional or digital form.

6. **More questions to ponder:** I have received wonderful feedback and provocative questions concerning the amount of time for lessons, adaptations, and of course assessment. I'm inviting you to continue pondering how we can move this framework more successfully into existing curriculum and program structures. I have provided a code for my website, www.angelamaiers.com, where you can share your questions and offer creative suggestions to other educators seeking to find ways of making this framework work.

Because you have *Classroom Habitudes* in your hands, I know you are moving beyond the rhetoric. I know you see your students as powerful thinkers capable of growing into scholars and leaders. Let the language of empowerment and opportunity ring through your classroom. Along with me, show the world that greatness is not a genetic predisposition but a position in which we can place all our students.

How to Get the Most Out of the Lessons

The main goal of this book and its supporting resources is to introduce you to a wide variety of ways and means to integrate the teaching of 21st century habits and skills through scaffolded interactive lessons for each of the seven habitudes: imagination, curiosity, self-awareness, perseverance, courage, passion, and adaptability. The lessons are designed for flexible use.

The habitudes instructional framework is designed to work seamlessly within almost any program structure or curriculum guidelines. Though most of the examples come from kindergarten through eighth-grade classrooms, you will find them easy to adapt and implement in high school classrooms and across alternative areas of study such as art, music, or physical education.

In the first chapter, I lay the groundwork for setting up the environment and procedures that prepare students for the habitudes conversations and studies. Once you feel that your students have a firm understanding of what a habitude is and its importance to their learning success, you can proceed with the lessons in a number of ways:

1. Select the habitude that fits your individual curricular objective.

    + Do you want to help students improve their reading, writing, and critical thinking skills? Begin with chapter 4 on self-awareness so you can relate it to your lessons on strategies.

+ Do you want to implement an inquiry-based science initiative? Chapter 3 on curiosity is filled with ideas and resources that support the power and practice of inquiry.

+ Do you want to enhance students' ability for solving mathematics problems? The lessons on adaptability in chapter 8 will definitely enhance their work in math.

+ Do you want to celebrate a students' artistic, musical, or creative contributions? The lessons on passion in chapter 7 would be a great place to start. Alternatively, you might want to focus on activities for imagination as presented in chapter 2.

2. Take one habitude at a time.

   There is no magic sequence or formula for studying the habitudes. Select a habitude that intrigues you or that you believe would be interesting for your students. The lessons are set up for conversations of fifteen to thirty minutes. Select a time in your schedule, and let students know you will be studying, for example, the habitude of imagination for the next three to four weeks. Each chapter is filled with a variety of lessons from which you can pick and choose. Additional resources in appendix A (page 129) can be used to create your own extended study.

3. Engage in an interdisciplinary study of the habitudes.

   Something quite powerful happens when every teacher the students meet tells them their habitudes count—that their success and happiness in mathematics, science, social studies, art, and reading will depend on their learning behaviors and mindsets. When teachers, as a team, announce they will be studying courage in each content area, the impact is grand. As students encounter examples of courageous historians, curious scientists and researchers, and imaginative writers and artists, their appreciation of the subject area and discipline is sure to deepen.

No matter which way you choose to proceed, the probability that students will begin making connections and envisioning the possibilities of their own imagination, curiosity, courage, and adaptability will increase.

The resources in the chapters will provide you with the necessary support and structure needed to make every lesson a success. I have provided the scope. I trust you with the sequence! I know these lessons work. I have seen lives changed in the process of this study. Whether you are helping students pass algebra or seeking to uncover their spirit of creativity, these lessons will improve their chances of success in ventures both big and small.

My greatest hope for the revised edition is for you to understand your own strength and power in students' lives. Many of your learners currently have or once had the habitudes but fail to see the potential of their own ability for public and private greatness. These students deserve to know that their passionate curiosity, powerful imaginations, and courageous abilities matter.

You are the only ones who can make that happen. Realizing that the habitudes matter will not be accomplished by following the scope and sequence correctly or covering every standard; knowing what matters happens when we share these conversations together. It will be your words that students will remember. And it will be your voice that conveys the notion of extraordinary.

Your Readiness to Teach the Habitudes

Think back to your initial thoughts when you read the Einstein quote at the beginning of this introduction (page 1). What impediments to learning do you think your students encounter? To what extent do you think education interferes with learning for today's students? Do you think that today's students are more in need of the habitudes than in years past?

In this context, I share a story from my friend David Armano, who reflected on his son's early experience in the current system of education. Figure I.1 is a worksheet that Max, David's son, proudly showed his dad.

Figure I.1: Max's Beep Beep! worksheet.

Source: Armano, 2006. Used with permission.

"Daddy, daddy! Look what I did!" Max said.

As any parent would, David replied, "That's awesome, Max!"

He was looking at the assignment, a worksheet that involved coloring and matching shapes. Typical stuff, he thought as his five-year-old skipped away. But upon closer examination, he couldn't help but notice the teacher's comments: "Good! Try staying in the lines."

David's subsequent thoughts were these:

> I understand that kids need to learn how to color in the lines. It teaches them basic coordination and concentration. But what does it teach them about themselves? What does it teach them about skills that might serve them well one day in the real world?
>
> Couldn't there be an assignment in addition to coloring shapes that maybe included handing them blank sheets of paper and asking them to invent and name a shape that no one has ever heard of before? Maybe some kid would come up with a Sqoval, or a Tri-square, or even an Octocircle. Who knows?
>
> The point is that we do need to be taught to do things like coloring shapes at a young age, but shouldn't we also be taught how to invent, create, and look at problems from a totally different perspective? (D. Armano, personal communication, fall 2009)

David's story perfectly illustrates what Einstein warned us of decades ago. Obedience, order, and sequence have become the laws of learning. Those who excel—our *good* students—diligently fall in line to prove they hear what we deliver, remember what we say, and answer what we ask. We operate from our scope and sequence, hoping the lessons and skills will be enough for our students to invent, create, collaborate, and solve their own problems. But deep down we understand exactly what David and Einstein were questioning; we know that eventually the demands of accountability, standardization, and conformity will keep most learners *within the lines*.

A 21st century classroom is within your reach. To reassure yourself that you are on the right path to teaching the habitudes, you might want to reflect on how the habitudes exist in your own life. The habitudes self-assessment exercise will help you do just that.

Our students have a chance at a different experience than you and I might have had. They have a chance to learn not only from our words but from our actions. We can and must be the learners we are expecting them to become.

Remember, your habitudes are what led you to open this book. Your desire to learn and grow is the best gift you can give to your students. Let's take this conversation to the classroom, shall we? You are one step closer to *yes*!

The Habitudes Self-Assessment

Examining how the habitudes exist in your life is a critical first step in your journey to make your students aware of the habitudes. This self-assessment will encourage you as you wrestle with three questions:

1. How do I define 21st century success?

2. Do I have the habitudes?

3. Do I extend my understanding of the habitudes to my students? How do I do this?

Your responses will reveal the habitude elements you are already using and will highlight areas for potential improvement. The assessment consists of twenty statements, which represent behaviors or attitudes that are characteristics of habitudes, and a scoring chart that shows how to interpret the results of your performance on the rating task (see fig. I.2). As you reflect on your performance, keep in mind that there are no right and wrong answers, no mastery, and no perfect score. There are new chances to learn and grow. Every day you have a chance to become a better learner and leader.

Directions: Use the five-point scale to assess your use of the habitudes. A rating of one indicates that you rarely use the habitude; a rating of five indicates that you use the habitude often. Add the tallies to get your habitude score.

Habitude Statement	Rating
I am confident in my abilities to succeed.	
I am not afraid to fail, and I try challenging things in which I know I will be uncomfortable or unskilled.	
I actively pursue different perspectives and fresh insights.	
I expect high-quality work from myself and others.	
When someone is upset, I try to understand how he or she is feeling.	
I can sell myself. I can articulate my unique strengths and talents with confidence.	
I am a go-getter, the first to try something new and different.	
I am highly motivated and driven.	
I am attuned to my team morale and the emotional state of my class.	
I can handle when things do not go as I have planned.	
I persevere in the face of obstacles.	
I am quick to adjust and adapt.	
I am passionately curious, always seeking new questions and avenues of thought.	

Figure I.2: My habitudes self-assessment.

continued→

Habitude Statement	Rating
I embrace and welcome change.	
My closest friends agree that I'm willing to acknowledge and learn from my mistakes.	
I take time to learn what people need from me so they can be successful.	
I'm optimistic about life. I can see beyond temporary setbacks and problems.	
I think that teams perform best when individuals learn new skills and challenge themselves, instead of perfecting the same tasks.	
Others would describe me as a leader.	
I am always learning or seeking to learn something new.	
My Score	

Score Range	What the Score Means About My Habitude Use
1–36	As leaders we must *show* the way, not simply tell our learners where to go and how to follow. In order to be an asset to others that you lead and serve, you will need to work on improving the mindset and perspective with which you approach the work. Examine the areas in which you have the highest points. Build on these existing strengths to move yourself into the next categories.
37–68	You're doing well, but it's likely that you can do more. You have the potential to do far better. While you've built the foundation of effective leadership, this is your opportunity to improve your skills and become the best you can be. Examine the areas where you lost points, and determine what you can do to develop skills in these areas.
69–100	Excellent! You're well on your way to becoming a transformative leader. However, you can never be too great or too experienced. Look at any of the areas where you didn't score maximum points, and figure out what you can do to improve your performance.

My Priorities for Improvement:

Visit **go.solution-tree.com/instruction** to download the handout *The Habitudes Self-Assessment*.

CHAPTER 1

Nurturing Genius: A Framework for Teaching and Learning the Habitudes

*Genius is misunderstood as a
bolt of lightning.*

—SETH GODIN

You can't settle for the ordinary when you comprehend you're extraordinary. I hope this statement will echo in your mind as you learn about the habitudes and use the lessons in this book with your students. Perhaps you have always been innately and overtly aware of the habitudes. For me, I remember my grandmother talking to me about the importance of hard work and perseverance, and hearing college professors quoting Edison, Einstein, and da Vinci. You too may have heard adages such as "Imagination is more important than knowledge" and "Success is one percent inspiration and 99 percent perspiration" (Edison as cited in Gelb, 2003, p. 313).

But did you live, embody, and study these principles of success in school? If your experience was anything like mine, these timeless lessons and practices were rarely talked about or nurtured during pre- or postgraduate years. In fact, I grew up believing that only a special *gifted* few could become extraordinary. Genius was presented as a rare gift—something in one's DNA rather than attributes that could be learned throughout one's life.

While I may have used one or more habitudes without realizing I was doing so, I can't help but wonder what my life and learning would have been like if I had been taught that imagination, curiosity, self-awareness, perseverance, courage, passion, and adaptability mattered. How different school would have been if only I had been told early on of my unique and genius qualities. In fact, this problem is centuries old—even Einstein and Edison were not recognized for the gifts they possessed. Imagine what they might have achieved with such self-knowledge. Our students deserve to be told early and often that they too were born with the potential for genius; ask any of their parents.

You may not know whether the future Steve Jobs or the next Shakespeare is sitting in your classroom. What can be confirmed is that learners who are told of and understand their unique abilities early on will most likely do the following:

- Excel at a different rate and pace
- Have a confidence about them that others can see immediately
- Be more equipped to maintain their optimism and confidence under stress
- Understand the need to rely on themselves more than others to get what they need in life
- Have greater potential for living a more productive and fulfilled life

The world has been changed by ordinary individuals who were blessed enough to have been encouraged and enabled to become extraordinary. Once you understand and believe that you are capable of the extraordinary, you will not settle for the ordinary. The same observation applies to your students. Once you have nurtured them in the habitudes, they will realize the strength of their capabilities to be imaginative, curious, self-aware, persistent, courageous, passionate, and adaptable. For this development to occur, we must understand and communicate four principles through our instruction:

1. All learners are capable of genius at one time or another. It is our responsibility to recognize that genius and use it in powerful and productive ways.

2. Learners must understand with specificity and depth the skills, competencies, and habitudes that differentiate extraordinary from the ordinary.

3. Learners must be willing to study, learn from, and be inspired by other genius thinkers across multiple disciplines and fields of study.

4. Learners must seek to identify, create, and be prepared to share their gifts with the world.

These principles serve as both foundation and structure in making the habitudes a part of our daily work and routines. I call this teaching and learning framework Name It, Claim It, Sustain It. However, before taking you through this instructional framework, I invite you to consider the idea of *genius* for a few minutes. Sharing a common definition and interpretation of this word is an important first step before we deconstruct the habitudes necessary for genius learning to occur.

Redefining Genius

Would all geniuses please raise your hands? Is your hand raised now? If not, consider why you *haven't* raised your hand high and proud. Why we are so averse to claiming our genius? What makes it so difficult to tap into and claim our own exceptional intelligence, creative power, and natural ability?

When I ask a room full of first graders, "Would all geniuses please raise your hand?" all hands fly up proudly. In a room of eighth graders or high school students, chances are no one will raise a hand, or a few will enthusiastically fire an arm into the air, setting off a round of laughter.

In his best-selling book *Linchpin*, author Seth Godin (2010) points out that we are all geniuses in our own ways. Godin's idea is not new. Ralph Waldo Emerson noticed it and wrote eloquently on the topic (Atkinson, 2002). Thomas Jefferson envisioned a society in which the genius of the individual was not circumvented by the crown or church. Twentieth-century change-makers like Gandhi, Margaret Mead, and Martin Luther King Jr. spoke to the transformative power of the individual, especially when the individual finds momentum in community. Despite this cultural heritage, we resist claiming genius because we find non-genius to be a safer place. This response is reinforced by an education culture that preaches standardization, conformity, and noncompetitiveness. From reading Godin and the views of others about genius, I have actively rethought my own definitions and interpretations of this concept. Godin's definition, presented in *Linchpin*, has been especially significant for me:

> Genius is the act of solving a problem in a way no one has solved it before. It has nothing to do with winning a Nobel prize in physics or attaining certain levels of schooling. It's about using human insight and initiative to find original solutions that matter. A genius is someone with exceptional abilities and the insight to find the not so obvious solution to a problem; a genius looks at something that others are stuck on and gets the world unstuck. (2010, chapter 1)

In other words—geniuses have the habitudes! Geniuses give, take, share, and grow by:

- Being diligently curious
- Using their imaginations in creative and powerful ways
- Facing fear in a challenging and courageous way
- Persevering with tenacity to overcome hurdles large and small
- Seeing inside themselves with a reflective honesty to use that awareness as an asset for growth
- Living and loving passionately

- Always understanding the importance of the work and their role in making it successful

Godin goes on to say that no one is or can be a genius all the time. For example, Einstein had trouble finding his house when he walked home from work every day. But all of us are geniuses sometimes, and we can be more often if we have a path to follow.

The Habitudes Instructional Framework

The Name It, Claim It, Sustain It framework is what I use to nurture and develop genius minds: learners who in their own way are capable of making their mark if they demonstrate and practice the habitudes. The framework is chronological but not linear; that is, the ability to name something is an important first step, followed by steps that enable ownership to develop—claiming and sustaining the concept. Each phase serves a specific purpose but can be revisited at any point within the teaching and learning cycle.

Phase One: Name It

In naming something, we bring meaning to it. In order for the habitudes to have real meaning in our students' lives, students must be able to talk about, describe, compare, and understand what the terms mean to them individually and collectively. This is why the Name It phase is crucial. It gives students a clear, concise, and consistent way of describing and defining success, and it supports their ability to differentiate the unique paths of achieving success.

What Is a Habitude?

Complete each of these statements, and then ask a friend or colleague to do the same. Compare your responses. In what ways are they alike or different? How does talking about your responses help you better understand the concepts?

Curiosity is . . .

The difference between curiosity and imagination is . . .

A learner demonstrates courage when . . .

To be adaptable is to be . . .

Visit **go.solution-tree.com/instruction** to download the handout *What Is a Habitude?*

As you may have suspected, this activity is not a simple task or a quick vocabulary exercise. Becoming comfortable talking about and describing the habitudes in detail will take time and effort. It is important to not to rush the Name It process. Take time to lead students through stories and examples of the habitudes in action. Be there to unpack the language and guide them as they attempt to create rich and detailed descriptions of these success traits. I encourage you not to feel self-conscious about sharing your own experiences with your students. In my work with students, I draw on my experiences to illustrate how the habitudes have contributed to and enriched my life.

I have developed four activities that you can use with your students in the Name It phase.

- Lesson One: Habitude Definitions
- Lesson Two: Habitude Word Storm
- Lesson Three: The Habitudes in Action
- Lesson Four: The Habitudes Posters

The activity shown in table 1.1 is an example of how you might develop your own definitions of the habitudes before you introduce students to the Name It phase of the instructional framework. By completing this exercise, you will gain an appreciation of what your students will do in their activities for defining the habitudes. This exercise can be easily adapted for use with students, as you will see in Lesson One.

Table 1.1: Definitions and Descriptions of the Habitudes

The Habitude	Definition	Image (Looks Like, Feels Like, Sounds Like)
Imagination is		
Curiosity is		
Self-awareness is		
Perseverance is		
Courage is		
Passion is		
Adaptability is		

Visit **go.solution-tree.com/instruction** to download the handout *Definitions and Descriptions of the Habitudes*.

Lesson One: Habitude Definitions

This activity provides students opportunities to talk with classmates about the meanings of the habitudes. The following is a description of my procedure for the activity.

I prepare a set of index cards containing the name of each habitude. I organize the students in pairs or small teams and have them select one card from the collection I have placed face down on a table. I give the students a few minutes to share their ideas about the meaning of the selected habitude. Next, I distribute the worksheet shown in table 1.2. I review the topics on the worksheet by asking the students to think about what the habitude looks like, feels like, and sounds like when someone exhibits it. Then I have the students share their ideas with the group. For a follow-up discussion with the whole class, I encourage students to consider these two questions:

1. How would you define this habitude?

2. When would be a good time or a bad time to use this habitude in learning?

Table 1.2: Defining the Habitudes

Habitude	What Is It?	Looks Like . . .	Sounds Like . . .	Feels Like . . .
1. Imagination				
2. Curiosity				
3. Self-Awareness				
4. Perseverance				
5. Courage				
6. Passion				
7. Adaptability				

Visit **go.solution-tree.com/instruction** to download the handout *Defining the Habitudes*.

Lesson Two: Habitude Word Storm

I suggest a strategy I call *word storming*. Like brainstorming, students will generate a collection of words, ideas, and phrases that convey the key meaning of a particular habitude. They then participate in a gallery walk to explore definitions of the habitudes that their classmates have developed.

I place seven pieces of chart paper—one for each habitude—around the room. (If you prefer, you can select fewer habitudes for a session and spread the activity over several days.) I have students form small teams. I direct each team to one of the habitude charts. I explain to the students that they will work together to brainstorm ideas about the habitude named on the chart paper. In addition to brainstorming words to describe the habitude, they can also use symbols, pictures, icons, or anything else to express their ideas. I allow each team about ten minutes to complete the word storm. When the teams have finished recording their descriptions, they participate in a gallery walk to see descriptions of the habitudes.

After the word storm and gallery walk have been completed, the class can begin discussing how they would define each of the seven habitudes.

Lesson Three: The Habitudes in Action

Games are a great way to further emphasize how the habitudes look in action. For instance, charades is a game everyone is familiar with. It requires many if not all of the habitudes: imagination, curiosity, adaptability, and so on.

For this activity, I place several games and brain teasers that relate to a particular habitude on tables around the room. I have students rotate in small groups to each table, taking ten to fifteen minutes to play the game or solve the puzzles. As students play, I remind them to consider the specific habitudes they used to play the game well. Once the students have explored the available games, I have them share with the whole group the habitudes they believe would be most beneficial in order to play the selected game.

Using Games to Understand the Habitudes in Action

- Pictionary™
- Guesstures™
- Mastermind™
- Risk™
- Life™
- Catch Phrase™
- Cranium™
- Chess
- Checkers
- Charades

Lesson Four: The Habitudes Posters

We're all aware that a picture is worth a thousand words. Creating mental images and graphic representations of those images are effective ways to help students develop and extend their understanding of terms and concepts (Marzano, Pickering, & Pollock, 2001). You might consider having the students add visual elements to their definitions. To get this activity started, I share the following descriptions of the habitudes with the students.

A Personal Visualization Exercise

Think of the words, images, phrases, and symbols that come to mind as you consider these descriptions of the habitudes.

Imagination: To a child, everyday unnoticed items can take on unique characteristics. For example, a cardboard box, a basket of unfolded laundry, and an individual blade of grass can become a fort, clothing

continued→

for a king and queen, and a harmonica that plays symphonic music, respectively. Imagination is not just for kids. Discovery, innovation, creativity, and learning all begin with imagination. Although the importance of imagination is undeniable, it's something we take away by forcing students to memorize and repeat rather than think and envision.

Curiosity: Champion learners are curious about everything. They ask questions and get involved in all stages of learning without worrying about the answer, instead relishing in the process. They have learned that by posing questions, they can generate interest and liveliness in the most exciting or mundane situation. This inquisitive attitude fuels their unrelenting quest for continuous learning.

Self-Awareness: We all have strengths and weaknesses in regard to our learning performance and capabilities. Knowing yourself as well as your strengths, preferences, and areas of need are critical characteristics of a successful learner. Yet self-awareness is more than just recognition of what you can or cannot be, do or do not have. This innate ability to stay in tune with yourself serves multiple purposes. Learners can foresee problems and use their strengths to overcome the difficulties they encounter.

Perseverance: I think of times in my life when it took more than *I think I can* to get me to my goal. Most recently, I ran in my first half marathon. Without resolve, determination, firmness, and endurance, I know I could not and would not have physically or mentally gone the distance.

Courage: Courageous learners understand that safety is risky. Success is the by-product of taking risks, closing our eyes, saying, "I will not let fear hold me back," and taking the plunge. I want students to understand that it takes courage to address the voices in their heads that echo doubts, questions, or other paralyzing thoughts.

Passion: Passion is not crazy, wacky, or even grand. It is not just for eccentrics or gurus; it is key to everyone's success. Passion is the energy, fuel, and drive needed for learners to keep going and provides the reasons that they will. At its deepest and most powerful level, our passion is a combination of hard thinking, creativity, and the need to dream big as we plan to pursue something that really matters.

Adaptability: Adaptability is more than just serving change; it is using change as an opportunity for growth. In fact, by anticipating change, you can control change. This kind of development requires robust adaptability. The world opens up for adaptable learners, as they approach each task and challenge willing to be a beginner. They approach their learning and life with a beginner's mindset. These learners embrace challenges with openness and flexibility.

From these descriptions, students can create graphic representations. I then show the students the Habitudes Posters (to see the posters, scan this code or go to http://sixhabitudes.wikispaces.com/file/detail/Untitled 1.tiff to download the file).

Habitudes Definition Assessment

The preceding activities provide students with many opportunities to acquire vocabulary to define the habitudes and to create images that are personally significant. You will know that your students are ready to move to the Claim It phase when they can use words and images to confidently complete the sentence completion task shown in table 1.1 (page 19) and the habitudes definition assessment shown in table 1.3.

Table 1.3: Habitude Definition Assessment

Teacher Reflection	Student Reflection
Imagination 1 ——+——+——+—— 5 *Because . . .*	Imagination 1 ——+——+——+—— 5 *Because . . .*
Curiosity 1 ——+——+——+—— 5 *Because . . .*	Curiosity 1 ——+——+——+—— 5 *Because . . .*
Self-Awareness 1 ——+——+——+—— 5 *Because . . .*	Self-Awareness 1 ——+——+——+—— 5 *Because . . .*
Perseverance 1 ——+——+——+—— 5 *Because . . .*	Perseverance 1 ——+——+——+—— 5 *Because . . .*
Courage 1 ——+——+——+—— 5 *Because . . .*	Courage 1 ——+——+——+—— 5 *Because . . .*
Passion 1 ——+——+——+—— 5 *Because . . .*	Passion 1 ——+——+——+—— 5 *Because . . .*
Adaptability 1 ——+——+——+—— 5 *Because . . .*	Adaptability 1 ——+——+——+—— 5 *Because . . .*

Visit **go.solution-tree.com/instruction** to download the handout *Habitude Definition Assessment*.

The habitudes definition assessment is designed to enable you and your students to reflect on what they have learned about the habitudes and what the habitudes mean in their lives. The assessment includes a five-point continuum—1 is low and 5 is high—on which you can mark where you fit in terms of your personal development of the selected habitude. Space is provided to explain the level selected on the continuum. Share the responses to the assessment with the class. Use these conversations to help students develop a common vocabulary to describe the habitudes.

Students' success in school and life depends on the extent to which they are able to engage in the habitudes. For additional information about the students' awareness of the habitudes, you may want to use the Habitude Actions Pre- and Postassessment presented in appendix B (page 139 or online at **go.solution-tree .com/instruction**). This assessment asks students to reflect on and respond to their habitude development by noting examples of situations in which they showed the habitude actions. The assessment has statements describing actions for each of the seven habitudes. The statements are exemplars that you can adapt for the age or grade level of students. The assessment can also be used as an observation checklist for you to evaluate your students' habitude development.

Phase Two: Claim It

The activities in the Name It phase enable the students to consciously label and describe the habitudes. From these activities and assessments, you and your students now have a common vocabulary to talk about each habitude. As a result, all of you are one step closer to claiming the habitudes in your lives and work.

To claim the habitudes, students must be able to relate and connect these attributes to specific individuals and behaviors. The Claim It phase starts with an immersion in a brief study of modern or historic individuals who embody the habitudes. This study has the potential to inspire students to emulate the habitudes they learn about from the lives of those individuals. These characters, living or otherwise, will serve as the role models for your students as they work toward understanding and acquiring the habitudes for themselves.

The Claim It phase culminates with the selection and assembly of a class Dream Team—a mutually agreed-upon team of individuals, each chosen for a specific habitude, who together represent the potential of ordinary individuals to accomplish extraordinary acts.

The Dream Team members and their habitudes will guide students in the process of improving their personal performance and will give them the confidence in the tasks and challenges they face because they know that others have faced the same.

As students develop strong contacts with the Dream Team members, studying their lives and accomplishments, they can begin to imagine themselves employing these techniques within their own learning and lives.

Here's what I say to get the conversation started.

I believe that each of us possesses the ability to achieve greatness in our lives. I also believe that each of us can learn a lot from individuals who have distinguished themselves by accomplishing something great and extraordinary.

I have been blessed in my own life to have encountered people who inspired me—people I consider in many ways to be special, intelligent, and brilliant. These extraordinary people have taught me by example in the ways they learn and lead.

Here's the amazing thing: I have never even met most of these people in person. I call these people my Dream Team. They are individuals I have deliberately selected to be inspired by and whose actions and behaviors I would like to reflect in terms of my own dreams and goals.

I have learned that you don't have to know people personally for them to be role models. Your Dream Team can include someone famously great, like Albert Einstein, or a special individual, a coach, or a teacher whom you want to be more like when you grow up. A good role model doesn't have to be someone famous or popular at the moment. A role model can be someone in your family, school, or community: someone whose actions you respect and whose behaviors and habits inspire you. But you may wonder how to identify such an individual. Here are some things you can think about as you select your role models:

- *What makes this individual interesting?*
- *What is special about this individual?*
- *Which habitude do you think this individual possesses? How do you know?*

I have designed an activity, the Dream Team Selection Procedure, that will help you identify one or more real-life mentors whom you may want to emulate. Write the answers, and put them away to review later.

The Dream Team Selection Procedure consists of four topics that encourage students to reflect on the qualities of individuals they consider for role models. For instance, the third topic asks them to identify one habitude that stands out for the selected individual. Here it is important for students to understand that, for example, Michael Jordan didn't win games because he was a great basketball player; he was a master of self-awareness and perseverance, which propelled his talent to a legendary level. You want students to recognize that it was Einstein's insatiable curiosity that changed the field of science. Similarly, if not for Walt Disney's audacious imagination, there would be no Disney World. To see a Dream Team lesson in action, go to www.angelamaiers.com/20/10/03/whos-on-your-dream-team.html or scan this code.

Here are the four Dream Team topics:

1. Create a list of ten people with whom you've achieved a kind of success or who have supported you in accomplishing something.

2. Next to each person's name, list the qualities you value most about that person. Be specific.

3. Reflect on all those qualities you've listed. Now select one key habitude that stands out above the others. Does this person stand out because of:

   + Imagination

   + Curiosity

   + Self-awareness

   + Perseverance

   + Courage

   + Passion

   + Adaptability

4. Next, select your top *two* choices to share with the class as the best possible candidates for the class Dream Team.

   The most important thing you need to be clear about is the reason you selected these people. You should know exactly what skills, behaviors, habits, or attitudes—the habitudes—you think make that individual extraordinary. For example, everyone knows that Albert Einstein was extraordinary. The important question to ask and answer is, What habitude did Einstein have that made him a genius?

To help the students organize their dream team ideas, I use a chart with the following headings:

- Person

- Qualities you most admire

- Key habitudes

(Visit **go.solution-tree.com/instruction** to download the handout *Dream Team Members*.)

Having students discuss and decide on a class Dream Team is an activity you may want to use as a culmination to the Claim It phase. In this activity, students can have lively discussions in which they present arguments in support of the individuals they want on the Dream Team. This experience should be both invigorating and inspiring for you and your students. The experiences students have in the Claim It phase will strengthen their understanding of the habitudes and awareness of how these play out in the lives of their role models. Claiming the habitudes is an essential step leading to the third phase of the habitude instructional framework.

Phase Three: Sustain It

The habitudes must be explicitly taught. This requires modeling, demonstration, reflection, collaboration, and lots and lots of practice. Through instruction and extended practice, awareness of the habitudes will move from something you do with the students to something that you seek for them to become. The habitudes offer students a path for their personal development—a path that leads them *to be*, *to do*, and *to have* what is needed for success in the 21st century.

The lessons in the chapters that follow are designed to support each of the phases in the instructional framework. Some of the lessons are lighthearted and fun, while others will require great courage and diligence to complete. In this series of lessons, students will discover their own genius and talent. As you and your students together explore each habitude, they will become aware of what success requires as well as understand the one or two habitudes that set them apart from the crowd.

The only path to expertise, as far as anyone knows, is practice. As soon as possible after each habitude lesson, encourage your students to experiment or practice the skill you are helping them develop. The sooner students are able to practice the habitude taught in the lesson, the more successful they will be in developing and applying the abilities to their own learning.

Are you ready to help students Name It, Claim It, and Sustain It? The lessons in chapters 2 through 8—the habitude chapters—are designed with this structure; however, I have used different headings for the phases to make the language more student friendly. The labels for the instructional framework and the comparable labels in the habitude lessons are shown as follows:

- *Name It* is identified as *The Pitch: Why [Habitude] Matters*.
- *Claim It* is identified as *The Anchor: The Million Dollar Conversation Starter*.
- *Sustain It* is identified at *Conversations That Last: Continuing the Dialogue*.

If you are still wondering how all this will work or if it will be possible to turn your classroom into a laboratory of innovation and creativity, I assure you that getting started is easier than you think. It begins simply by recognizing the genius already exists.

I leave you with a final thought inspired by Seth Godin's (2010) book *Linchpin*: You are a genius, and the world needs your contribution. Imagine you are a student walking into a classroom, and this is the first thing you see and the last words you hear from your teacher. How would that change things for you? The words we use with our students may have long-lasting impacts on the way they think about themselves, about their teachers, and about school in general (Brisco, Arriaza, & Henze, 2009; Denton, 2007; Farrell, 2009; Johnston, 2004).

See firsthand how starting our days in service of our students' genius changes everything! You will find more ideas about nurturing student genius and what other teachers have done to foster genius behaviors in their students at these sites (or search www.angelamaiers.com for Nurturing Genius):

Begin here, and the rest will fall into place—I promise.

Reflections

The chapters that follow spell out specific lessons and resources for introducing the habitude conversations into your lesson plans. I realize that it might not be realistic to expect a habitude lesson in every classroom every day, but the following sets of questions can help you think about how the habitudes fit into the learning and lives of you and your students throughout the year.

The questions posed in this section are designed to provide you with some space in which you can consider the habitudes in your own personal and professional development.

What Is Education? Why Are We Here?

- Who am I teaching?
- What do I want most for my students to know and be able to do?
- Who currently teaches these skills, values, and habits of heart and mind?
- How will I judge the success of my teaching?
- What will students remember most about their time in my classroom and with me?
- What legacy do I wish to leave?

How Do Classroom Design and Atmosphere Affect Learning?

- What is the first thing students will notice about my classroom?
- What do I want them to notice and remember?
- How do I want my students to interact in my classroom?
- In what ways will students need to interact in order to understand and embrace the habitude conversations to come?

- What resources should be available for my students to be successful in their study of these 21st century skills?

- How can I use the space we have to build community, culture, and a more trusting relationship?

How Does My Teaching Affect My Students?

- What is the most important thing that I tried to teach my students this week?

- How did I accomplish this?

- How will this knowledge impact their current and future learning?

- What was the greatest lesson I learned from my students?

CHAPTER 2

Imagination

Imagination is more important
than knowledge.
— ALBERT EINSTEIN

What is imagination? How does imagination work? Can it be taught? If so, how do we go about doing that? These are the kinds of questions philosophers and theorists have spent centuries pondering and ones I seek to answer for this critically important habitude.

Imagination is the foundation of all thinking. Rorty (2000) observed that human imagination has no limits and words alone cannot do it justice. Philosophers, poets, novelists, playwrights, and scientists have written about imagination and its effects on people and their lives. As Heaney (1995, p. xv) says, "The imaginative transformation of human life is the means by which we can most truly grasp and comprehend it." Imagination enables us to create and renew experiences and gives us the freedom to envision how things might or could be (Spencer, 2002). Imagination has been defined and associated with the ability to form images, store memories, create illusions, and visualize new realities. Let's review the definition of the habitude of imagination:

> Imagination is the mind's ability to constantly create images containing thoughts and memories ignited from our senses. In those images, we create our ideals, role models, heroes, loves, concepts, perceptions, and ideas on how to thrive and survive.

Life is exactly what we imagine it to be. So, let's explore with students how far their imaginations can take them.

The Pitch: Why Imagination Matters

There are only three pure colors: red, blue, and yellow. But look at how Michelangelo imagined these colors into majestic art. There are seven musical notes, yet hear what Chopin, Vivaldi, and Mozart created from them. Imagination is the active ingredient in making all this happen.

If we cannot see the possibility, we cannot achieve the outcome. Imagination is our mind's eye and gives us the capacity to jump from present facts to future possibilities. Our capacity to dream, hope, and plan for the future is influenced and impacted by the control and understanding of imagination's remarkable power. Imagination serves us in many ways:

- Imagination helps us learn about ourselves and the world around us.

- Imagination helps us cope with and solve problems.

- Imagination helps us become more creative.

- Imagination makes it possible to experience a whole world inside the mind, enabling one to mentally explore both past and future.

The following conversations will help prepare students to draw from their imaginations and intellect in creative ways, today and every day for the rest of their lives.

The Anchor: The Million-Dollar Conversation Starter

I like to greet students at the start of a lesson: for example, "Good morning, boys and girls," or "Good afternoon, everyone," or "Hello, passionate learners." I think conversational greetings are important when working with students. No doubt, you have favorite forms of greeting that you use with your students.

Here's what I say to students when I start the conversation about imagination:

Two words are important to learning: knowledge *and* imagination.

What do you think is the relationship between these two words?

At this point, I give students time to talk and discuss the relationship between *knowledge* and *imagination*.

I continue the conversation as follows:

Knowledge is what we know. Knowledge represents what we have learned and mastered.

Imagination is how we use our knowledge and experiences to envision the future. Imagination allows us to see life as it would or could be. Here is what Albert Einstein said about the two: "Imagination is more important than knowledge itself."

Why do you think Einstein felt that way? Do you agree?

At this point, I allow the students to engage with each other in conversation, creating a community of imaginative learners. Remember, collaboration plus competition can equal greater creativity. After students have had a few minutes to share their ideas with peers, I continue the conversation.

Successful learning is more than just absorbing and remembering information. Understanding in school and in our lives requires many different parts of our imaginations. In fact, imagination is so important it has been called the most essential tool for human intelligence. Here's why: with it we can invent new realities.

As we explore the habitude of imagination together over the next days and weeks, we are going to be learning about tools important and related to imagination: imaging, visualizing, creating, and innovating. With these tools there is no limit to what our imaginations can do.

Think about this for a minute:

Everything new, every invention, every idea, every improvement in our life comes from our imagination—not from our knowledge!

It's not so long ago there were no cars, no airplanes, no Internet, and, yes, no video games! All these groundbreaking revolutions started with the power of the human imagination—not human knowledge! Until someone imagined it, none of the things you know and use were real.

Today, we are going to explore this amazing thing we call our imagination by taking a look at how it works and how using it wisely can help you improve your life in school and out. Are you ready to do that? Now, relax and close your eyes. Use your imagination and try to form a picture in your mind of the following scene. Listen carefully to the way I prompt and prod your imaginations to help you get the image as clear as possible.

You are a part of a team of world-famous mountain climbers, and you have just reached the peak of Mount Everest. You have attempted this dangerous and challenging climb twice before and failed. After seven long, grueling weeks, you are there! Put yourself in that spot, right at the very peak! Can you see yourself there? Keep your eyes closed. Focus and visualize yourself standing there.

I am going to challenge you to really concentrate. What are you wearing? What does the equipment on your back feel like after climbing all that way? Feel your arms and legs—how would you describe them? How about your face? Can you see your breath? Take a deep breath in and describe the smells. Now listen; what do you hear? What are your teammates saying? How do their voices sound? What emotions are you experiencing? How would you describe those feelings? Stay really still; freeze that moment in your mind.

Okay, now open your eyes. How do you feel? Anyone exhausted? What sense was strongest for you? What made the image most clear and most real?

I make sure to ask questions about the senses without directing which sense students should feel most. Everyone has different sense strength, so let the imagination flow and grow. I continue with another description that invites the students to use their imaginations.

Now let's try something a little less strenuous. I call this the lemon test. It goes something like this:

Imagine you're in a kitchen and there's a bowl of fresh lemons. You take one and place it on a chopping board and slice it open. Can you smell that fresh, lemony fragrance as it sweeps up to your nose and spreads across the entire room? Slowly pick up the lemon and open your mouth . . . that's right . . . and squeeze in a huge mouthful of juice.

Can you taste it?

At this point in the lesson, I can clearly see their puckering faces and know for sure their taste buds are working. I ask the students to think about these simple exercises we have shared.

What did we learn about the power of our imaginations today?

Your imagination may be all in your head, but its effects can be felt all throughout your body. Don't you agree? I hope you say yes!

Here are some things I would like us to consider and reflect on for tomorrow:

- *What did you learn about your imagination today?*
- *How can having a good imagination influence your learning?*
- *How do you use your imagination now?*

Conversations That Last: Continuing the Dialogue

Imagination cannot be mastered. It develops over time and with practice. The following imagination lessons provide you with specific ideas and tools to build imagination. These lessons do not follow a prescribed scope and sequence. They can and should be expanded and extended over days and weeks. These conversations keep the habitude alive and moving so students can link imagination in their school work and their life work. I have designed three lessons to help students learn more about imagination and how to use it. The lessons are:

1. Connecting creativity and imagination
2. Imagining and storing success moments
3. Imagining and solving problems

Lesson One: Connecting Creativity and Imagination

The accomplishments of famous people can be used to show the connection between creativity and imagination. For example:

- Galileo made his first important scientific observation at age seventeen.
- Handel composed music when he was eleven years old.
- Concert singer Marian Anderson began her singing career at age six, teaching herself how to play the piano at age eight.

Incredible discoveries and achievements have been made by people in their early years and teens. Right now, our students' brains are ripe and ready to create new and brilliant ideas, so this is a great time to talk to them about things that will enhance their imaginative and creative abilities.

After greeting the students, I begin the lesson as follows.

Today I want to talk to you about creativity and its link to using your imagination in productive and powerful ways. Creativity involves your ability to take the thoughts and ideas you imagine and turn them into something you want. You already are creative. Do you remember when you were younger and could take an ordinary cardboard box and turn it into a fort? Or take a bathroom towel, become a superhero, and fly around your house? That is creativity and imagination at work.

Creativity doesn't stay strong without work and commitment. Like any other mental process, it takes practice to get good at it. Believe it or not, one of the best ways to get your imaginative and creative juices going is to play a game. Games are one of the best tools creative people use to come up with their ideas. Creative playing leads to creative thinking and often to creative results. Sometimes adults forget to let you know the importance of playfulness, messing around, and trying out new ideas just for the fun of it! Some grownups have lost their creative spirit, but I know you all have not. So let's play for a bit, shall we? This game is called How Come?

Here's how it works. I'm going to describe a situation or setting. Your task is to answer the question How come? with as many creative scenarios as your imagination will allow. Push yourself to stretch your ideas beyond the obvious.

Here's the situation:

Mrs. Maiers went to a school in the middle of the day, in the middle of the week, but she didn't see any children there. How come?

Certain games and puzzles can furnish your students with plenty of opportunity to flex their creative muscles. Games like chess and checkers are great as they both force students to map out strategies and make moves that depend on what an opponent would do. Interactive games like Cranium, Pictionary, and Guesstures provide great creative exercise in thinking up novel ways to communicate and compete.

Lesson Two: Imagining and Storing Success Moments

I use the following comments to focus the students' attention on using imagination for remembering successful events in their lives.

Much of our thinking starts with a memory. It can be a memory from a moment ago (a reaction) or a memory from our past (a reflection). We keep our memories in imaginary storage file boxes and folders.

The key to success is knowing how to find the right memory file and pull it up at the right time.

We are going to do two things today:

1. *Create a success file*
2. *Practice using this file for future goals*

In the next section of this lesson, I ask students to think of a time when they displayed courage and strength.

Think about a special time when you were courageous and strong. You were awesome. You were confident. You shined like a star.

I have the students spend the next ten to fifteen minutes writing, talking, drawing, and sharing details with one another about the event. When I think they have captured every detail, I give a standard file folder to each student. I continue the lesson as follows.

Now that we have filled our minds with the most fantastic memories of success, we want to make sure those memories are firmly planted in our imaginations. We can do this by keeping a record of our successes. Take the file folder and in large letters write your name—for example, Angela's Success Story.

You will now be able to take this built-in success folder out anytime you find yourself facing a challenging task. This is where your imagination is critical. You will need to imagine that moment over and over. The more times you can experience that moment, the more successful you will be.

Try pulling out this file the next time you are about to face a challenge. Instead of worrying, imagine and relive this past success experience when you excelled. Think of how creative, courageous, and wonderful you were. Relive every detail of the event. Use that moment to give yourself confidence and security. You rocked then, and you can and will do the same in your new situation.

I have done this activity many times for myself, and I promise it works. My success file has changed everything for me. Now I work to add more files so I will have many memories to choose from. Every positive and successful moment of your life and learning can and should be stored for later access.

Let's start making your first success memory now!

Lesson Three: Imagining and Solving Problems

One should not put pencil to paper before having visualized what one wants from all angles . . . I have come to work by a series of mental images . . . the drawing board enables me to give effects to those images.
—ETORE BUGATTI

I tell the students that we are going to have a conversation about the problems we face. I tell them that Bugatti was a famous sports car designer and manufacturer who knew how to use his imagination to solve problems. I share Bugatti's quote with the class. The conversation is as follows.

Today's conversation is about the problems we face. The fact is, everyone has problems. They can be small things like, What shoes am I going to wear today? (This is actually a common problem for me.) Or, How am I going to get this assignment done by Friday? (Perhaps this is a common problem for you.) Luckily, you have what you need to solve almost any problem. You guessed it—your brain and your powers of imagination. Successful problem solving takes more than gathering information. It requires looking at the problem from many different angles, upside down and inside out.

Finding imaginative solutions to the challenges and difficulties is not an easy task. We will practice this together often. The work we do will not only help in school but will also become a strength for you long after our conversations are over. Being a successful problem solver is one of the most important skills you will use outside of school.

Here's what I see happening often, even with grownups. When confronted with a problem, people often try to force their brain into coming up with a solution right away. I am going to model for you a better system for working through problems using the powers of your imagination.

The system I use is called mind mapping *[Buzan, 2010]. Mind mapping is a tool that maps out the things that I am imagining would be or could be. In a mind map, I can contain all the elements of a problem in a single visual take. It allows me to see the color, shape, and sound of my problem and its possible solutions.*

Let me show you how it works. I follow three steps:

1. *I start with the problem; it is my central image.*

2. *I create the branches to represent possible solutions.*

3. *I share my mind map with others so that as we talk they can add branches that stretch and grow my thinking as well [see fig. 2.1, page 38].*

Imaginative problem solving does not make my problems and challenges disappear, but it does allow me to see problems in a different ways. Each time I work out a problem in this way, my thinking and my brain get stronger. I am able to tackle bigger problems with more efficiency and confidence knowing there is always more than one way of working it out.

For more information about mind mapping and resources to develop mind maps, go to www.businesscreditcards.com/bootstrapper /the-mindmapping-toolbox-100-tools-resources-and-tutorials/ or scan this code.

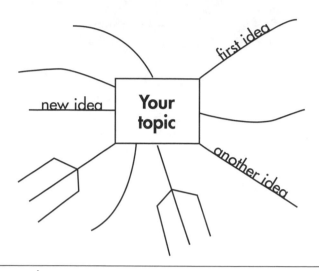

Figure 2.1: Mind map template.

Student Habitude Reflection

Students can respond to these prompts for reflection on imagination in their habitude notebooks.

My Reflections on Imagination

When I close my eyes, the first thing I remember about learning is . . .

I use my imagination to help me . . .

Using my imagination makes me feel . . .

Who is the most imaginative person I know or have read about? A technique the individual uses to stay imaginative and creative is . . .

I believe I am imaginative because I . . .

Visit **go.solution-tree.com/instruction** to download the handout *My Reflections on Imagination*.

Chapter Takeaway

We tend to think imagination is child's play, yet in reality, every human being has an imagination. Although it may be repressed, inactive, or distorted, it exists. When people are asked about their imagination, many may reply they have none; others will claim they have too much. Some might say they lost theirs long ago. When we talk to our students about their imaginations, let's ask not whether they have one (because they do), but rather what they are going to do with it.

Although I haven't included reflection comments for every lesson in this book, I routinely use questions to help myself think about what happened in lessons. Here is an example of the questions I used to reflect on how the students performed with the How Come? game (page 35):

- Did the students persist until all possible scenarios were explored?
- Were they able to get past the common answers of a spring break or fire drill?
- How soon did they come up with the far out answers such as alien invasions?
- Which students first came up with different kinds of schools—like night school or a school of fish?

Reflections

Imaginative students need imaginative teachers. An important step in developing this habitude in our students is to embrace our own imaginative potential, allowing ourselves to be creative.

The following reflection questions are intended to give you a window into your own creative spirit:

- In what ways are you creative?
- Do you spend time with other creative people?
- Do you play, laugh, and use humor to enhance experiences? Do you fantasize?
- Do you express your own creative talents? Do you paint, cook, sew, write . . . ?
- Do you daydream by just letting your mind wander?
- Do you make up similes and metaphors?
- Do you pay attention to small ideas that might someday become big?
- Do you take yourself out of your comfort zone?

Imagination Resources for Students

Bang, M. (1991). *Picture this: Perception and composition*. New York: Bulfinch Press.

Carter, D. (2005). *One red dot*. New York: Little Simon.

Desimini, D. (2004). *My beautiful child*. New York: Blue Sky Press.

Gonsalves, R., & Thomson, S. L. (2003). *Imagine a night*. New York: Atheneum Books.

James, B. (2004). *My chair*. New York: Levine Books.

Johnson, C. (1998). *Harold and the purple crayon*. New York: HarperCollins.

Keats, E. J. (1996). *The snowy day*. New York: Viking.

Lehman, B. (2006). *Museum trip*. Boston: Houghton Mifflin.

Marzollo, J. (1998). *Close your eyes*. New York: Puffin Books.

Messenger, N. (2005). *Imagine*. New York: Walker Books.

Modesitt, J. (1993). *Mama, if you had a wish*. New York: Green Tiger Press.

Radunsky, V. (2004). *What does peace feel like?* New York: Atheneum Books.

Reynolds, P. H. (2004). *The dot*. New York: Walker Books.

Rylant, C. (1994). *All I see*. New York: Scholastic.

Shannon, D. (2004). *Alice the fairy*. New York: Scholastic.

Shaw, C. G. (1998). *It looks like spilt milk*. New York: HarperCollins.

Thomson, S. L. (2005). *Imagine a day*. New York: Atheneum Books.

Sendak, M. (1963). *Where the wild things are*. New York: Harper & Row.

Wilson, J. (2000). *Imagine that!* Toronto, ON: Fitzhenry & Whiteside.

Yolen, J. (2003). *Color me a rhyme*. Honesdale, PA: Boyds Mills Press.

Imagination Resources for Teachers

Buzan, T., & Keene, R. (1994). *Buzan's book of genius and how to unleash your own*. London: Stanley Paul.

de Bono, E., & Weidenfeld, G. (1976). *The great thinkers*. New York: Putnam.

Gardner, H. E. (1994). *Creating minds: An anatomy of creativity as seen through the lives of Freud, Einstein, Picasso, Stravinsky, Eliot, Graham, and Gandhi*. New York: Basic Books.

Gardner, H. (2009). *Five minds for the future*. Cambridge, MA: Harvard Business School Press.

Harrison, S. (2006). *Ideaspotting: How to find your next great idea*. HOW Books.

Kosslyn, S. M. (1996). *Image and brain: The resolution of the imagery debate*. Cambridge, MA: Massachusetts Institute of Technology Press.

Pinker, S. (1999). *How the mind works*. New York: Norton.

Vendler, Z. (1985). *The matter of minds*. New York: Oxford University Press.

Weisberg, R. W. (1993). *Creativity—beyond the myth of genius*. New York: Freeman.

CHAPTER 3
Curiosity

Curiosity is one of the most permanent and
certain characteristics of a vigorous intellect.
— SAMUEL JOHNSON

Who would want to be without curiosity? Great minds are curious. You would be hard pressed to find an intellectual giant who was not: Thomas Edison, Leonardo da Vinci, Albert Einstein, and Richard Feynman were all curious characters.

Yet I wonder . . .

- Why do some students end up more curious than others?

- How can we add curiosity to our teaching toolbox and our conversations regarding teaching and learning?

- How can we live more curious lives ourselves as we model for our students what living a curious life is like?

This chapter seeks to explore answers to these questions. The lessons will help develop and nurture students' curious instincts as they work consciously on their habitude of curiosity.

Before considering the lessons, let's review the definition of the habitude of curiosity:

> Curiosity is a mindset that enables individuals to explore their internal and external worlds by asking questions, seeking answers, and engaging in a wide range of personal and interpersonal activities.

The proverb "curiosity killed the cat, but satisfaction brought it back" may offer an important theme for your students. Developing the habitude of curiosity has the potential to enhance their lives in many ways, not the least of which is the satisfaction that comes with learning new things about themselves and the world around them. Curiosity lessons can be eye openers for your students.

The Pitch: Why Curiosity Matters

Without a doubt, curiosity is a trait of genius minds, but why is curiosity so important to our students and their learning? In working with students, I like to have them think about how being curious makes life more interesting; for example:

- Curiosity keeps the brain active and awake.
- Curiosity keeps us open and ready for new ideas.
- Curiosity keeps life and learning exciting.

What if and *I wonder* are expressions that keep our brains in motion. Curious brains are active brains, and active brains become smart brains. Like any muscle, the mind becomes stronger with exercise. Curious people live full and adventurous lives as each new quest and question leads them down roads otherwise not traveled. So let the questions begin!

The Anchor: The Million-Dollar Conversation Starter

I want this first conversation with kids to be clear and specific about what curiosity is and how it is important in their lives. I prepare an anchor chart, What Is Curiosity?, on which I can record students' thoughts and responses to the question. I also prepare a selection of quotations about curiosity from well-known people. I write individual quotations on pieces of paper that I distribute to the students as they work in small groups. I supply chart paper for each group to record their ideas about the quotation.

I greet the students and tell them our lesson today is about curiosity and the role being curious plays in their learning. I ask, What does curiosity mean to you?

To keep thinking active and public, I use the anchor chart to record students' thoughts and responses to the question. A sampling of responses from kindergarten children follows.

Kindergartners' Ideas About Curiosity

Curiosity means . . .

- You have to ask a lot of questions
- You are really excited about learning
- You think about stuff you are reading and learning and wonder about it
- You discover answers to things you want to find out more about
- Learning about things you love

- The teacher wonders what you want to know about a topic, and then she puts your questions under the "W" of the chart (What I Know, What I Want to Learn, What I Learned strategy)
- Having tons of questions in your brain
- Thinking hard
- I am not exactly sure, but I think it has something to do with school—it could be a good thing?!

When all thoughts of curiosity are captured on the chart, I invite students to hear what others have said about the topic. I continue the conversation by saying:

Thank you so much for sharing your thoughts and ideas about curiosity with me. I thought you might be interested in hearing what others have said about curiosity. I have collected several famous quotes about curiosity and the importance of living a curious life.

As you work in small groups today, I am going to provide each group with a famous quote and a piece of chart paper to record your thinking on. As you read what these famous voices are saying about curiosity, I'd like you to consider and respond to three questions:

1. *How is this person defining curiosity?*
2. *How did curiosity benefit this person as a learner?*
3. *What is being said about curiosity that we can apply in our lives?*

Quotes can be collected from any specific field or discipline. A few to get you started follow.

Quotes About Curiosity From Famous People

The desire to know is natural to good men.—Leonardo da Vinci

Curiosity is one of the permanent and certain characteristics of a vigorous mind.—Samuel Johnson

Judge a man by his questions rather than by his answers.—Voltaire

Curiosity is the very basis of education and if you tell me that curiosity killed the cat, I say only the cat died nobly.—Arnold Edinborough

The important thing is not to stop questioning. Curiosity has its own reason for existing.—Albert Einstein

Never lose a holy curiosity.—Albert Einstein

Wisdom begins in wonder.—Socrates

Curiosity must be kept alive. One must never, for whatever reason, turn his back on life.—Eleanor Roosevelt

continued→

> The greatest virtue of man is perhaps curiosity. —Anatole France
>
> Curiosity is lying in wait for every secret. —Ralph Waldo Emerson
>
> Mere curiosity adds wings to every step. —Goethe

Students write, draw, and discuss their reactions and responses to the quote on their chart paper. Each chart is displayed around the room, creating a *quote wall*. Students can walk around the room with group members, adding their additional reactions and perspectives to each quote.

The conversation culminates with powerful discussions of the value and necessity of individuals to tap into and develop their own curiosity habitude. I use several questions to facilitate students' self-reflection and application of our curiosity conversation to their own learning lives.

- What are you most curious about?
- What subjects in school are you most interested in?
- What is it about those subjects that most interests you?
- If you could study or investigate any topic, what would it be?
- How does your curiosity affect how you approach a topic? A text? How hard you may work or how you feel?

I keep the charts posted so students can refer to them during other lessons about curiosity.

Conversations That Last: Continuing the Dialogue

Curiosity cannot be mastered. It develops over time and with practice. The following curiosity lessons provide you with specific ideas and tools to build students' curiosity, develop their capabilities to ask questions, and create opportunities for self-reflection.

These lessons do not follow a prescribed scope and sequence. They can and should be expanded and extended over days and weeks. These conversations keep the habitude alive and moving, enabling students to link curiosity to their work at school and to their lives.

Lesson One: Building Curiosity

According to Mihaly Csikszentmihalyi (2002), a direct relationship exists between attention and our interest in the world. In other words, nothing is interesting to us unless we pay attention to it. Rocks are not interesting until we begin collecting them. People in the mall are not interesting until we become curious about their lives. Vacuum cleaners are not interesting until we need a new one. According to Csikszentmihalyi, we can develop our curiosity (and fight boredom) by making a conscious effort to build it by paying attention.

To test Csikszentmihalyi's theory in the classroom, I give students the following curiosity challenge: *Think of a topic you have studied or are studying that you believe is the* most *uninteresting.*

Apologies are due to science and math teachers, for some of most immediate responses include rocks, molecules, and fractions. The good news is that we can turn the uninteresting into interesting and find relevance in any topic if we make a conscious effort to direct our attention and questions toward that topic.

Let's see how it goes. Have students pick a subject, focus on curiosity, and turn the subject inside out and upside down.

Tenth-Grade Students Focus Their Curiosity on Rocks

Here is what we asked when we looked at rocks through a curiosity lens:

- How many kinds of rock have been identified?
- What if we could turn all rock into fuel?
- How many uses are there for rock?
- What rock has been the most valuable?
- Who invented that saying "harder than a rock"?
- How does rock turn into diamonds or other jewels?
- Where can I find the largest rock?
- When climbers climb rock, how do they hold on?
- How many injuries have occurred because of rocks?
- Are there still rock slides in America?
- Has anyone ever died from a rock slide?
- Why is gravel cheap rock?
- Is volcanic rock softer than normal rock?
- When does a rock turn into a mountain?

Depending on the age group you are working with, the responses from the students might be quite different.

Second Graders Focus Their Curiosity on Rocks

Through their curiosity lens, second-grade students wondered about rocks in this way:

- Do rocks matter to nature, or are they just there?
- What is the oldest rock?
- How are rocks formed?
- Are there new kinds of rocks being created today?
- Is there anything in the world that is harder than a rock?
- What makes the colors in rocks?
- When rocks form, how long does that take?
- What is the difference between a rock and a mineral?
- Do other planets have rock like Earth?
- What makes some rocks smooth?
- What are the biggest rock collections in the world?
- What is the softest and what is the hardest rock?
- Is a cliff just one big rock?

How about your students? What would their topics be? How would they respond?

After the exercise, it's time to reflect with students about the experience of using curiosity to turn a subject they were not excited about into something worthy of their time and attention. I ask the students:

- *Was being curious worth it?*
- *In what way did being intentionally curious change how you felt about the topic we were studying?*
- *How did paying attention in this way make the topic more interesting?*
- *How did having others around help?*
- *What challenges still remain?*

These questions ignite great conversations about future learning and behavior, as not everything we read or learn will be of interest to our brains. Demonstrating to students their own ability to turn the uninteresting into the interesting—and yes, even have fun in the process—is invaluable.

Encourage your students to test this theory in other aspects of their lives as well. Challenge them to be purposefully curious outside the classroom. So the next time they are at the grocery store, in the car, or even watching TV, encourage them to notice, really notice, and ask questions—just because they can!

While you are encouraging your students to be curious, you might begin to analyze your own level of curiosity.

Personal Curiosity Inventory

1. Did you grow up being very curious about the world, the way things work, and other people?

2. What experiences have you had that fostered or inhibited your curiosity?

3. Who were your role models of curiosity?

4. Reflect on the last book you read or project you completed; what intrigued you most?

5. What questions do you have now?

Visit **go.solution-tree.com/instruction** to download the handout *Personal Curiosity Inventory*.

Lesson Two: Building Questioning Tools

Curiosity fuels our imagination. Our wonderment serves as a prerequisite to the questions we ask. In this lesson, I want students to see how curiosity and questioning go hand in hand. I have used two books that do a great job of showing students the way curious minds work by using questions as tools for powerful thinking and learning. *Where Do Balloons Go?* (Curtis, 2000) works wonderfully for starting this conversation with younger students; *The Wise Woman and Her Secrets* (Merriam, 1999) ignites powerful dialogue with older students. Both texts feature main characters whose curiosity and wonder about the world spark in them a plethora of questions.

Before introducing the stories, I ask kids to think about curious people they know or have read about:

- *How do you know they are curious?*

- *What about them tells you they are curious?*

As students share examples and descriptions of curious people, they will see that a hallmark of curious minds is the capacity and capability to ask lots of questions. As we explore the characters in the text, I encourage students to look for evidence that the main character is curious or exhibits curious behavior. Students see that curious characters, both in books and in life, use questions to awaken, explore, and sustain their curiosity.

To applaud and practice asking questions as a way to embrace and enhance curiosity, I ask students to collect the questions that are most important to them in a special box or container. These wonder boxes help students initiate and track their inquiries about topics they are passionate and curious about.

I give students the opportunities to explore their wonder box topics and questions in their reading and learning. From time to time I am able to take them though the entire inquiry cycle, demonstrating how expert learners are able to find answers to questions they feel most curious and convicted about. An example of a curiosity lesson is available by visiting http://sixhabitudes .wikispaces.com/curiosity or scanning this QR code.

Lesson Three: Asking Genius Questions

Our students start life like Einstein: with curiosity and an insatiable desire to learn. As time goes on, students grow to believe that answers are more important than the questions. This lesson puts the emphasis and importance back on the skill of questioning. Here's my conversation with the students:

> *Do you agree with the following statement?* Thinking is a process of asking and answering questions. *(Say yes!) If we want to change the quality of our thinking, then we must look carefully at the kinds of questions we are asking.*

> *One of the most powerful thinkers in history was Albert Einstein. He was not only passionately curious, but he also knew the importance of asking powerful questions. What made Einstein stand out were the kinds of questions he asked. He did not just look at a problem or a text and ask who, what, where, when, and how. Einstein's questions were different and numerous.*

> *Now, here is the good news. The power to think at this high level is not just reserved for genius minds. We can learn from Einstein. Today we are going to practice thinking like Einstein using his questioning state of mind to help us explore our topic. We are going to practice asking one another genius-level questions. To help us, I've created a deck of question cards. I call them Q-cards. The Q-cards have questions that Einstein and other genius minds might ask if they were here exploring this topic with us.*

> *The most important thing about this exercise is to keep asking questions. Don't worry about finding the answers, just keep asking. Our brains have Einstein power. Are we ready to use them wisely? Let's make Einstein proud.*

I want students to leave this experience reflecting on the nature and purpose of their questions. To guide their reflections, I ask the following questions:

- *Which question do you think was most genius?*
- *Which question are you most proud of?*

- *What kind of questions did you hear yourself asking often?*
- *What is another question you might now ask yourself?*

This lesson works well when I divide students into small groups, giving each group its own deck of genius questions. The questions I use are shown in figure 3.1.

What if . . . ?	Is . . . the reason for . . . ?
I wonder why . . .	Can . . . ?
If . . . ?	Would you rather . . . ?
What is it that . . . ?	What would it take to . . . ?
When is it . . . ?	Why is it like that . . . ?
Who could . . . ?	How is . . . like . . . ?
Is it possible to . . . ?	If I . . . , could . . . ?
When is . . . ?	Does it matter if . . . ?
What could happen if . . . ?	How can . . . ?
If it were possible . . . ?	What is your opinion about . . . ?
Are there . . . ?	Is it right to . . . ?
Why is . . . ?	I wonder when . . .
How . . . ?	I'm wondering if . . . ?
Where did . . . ?	How could it . . . ?
Do you . . . ?	Why are . . . ?

Figure 3.1: Genius questions.

Visit **go.solution-tree.com/instruction** to download the handout *Genius Questions*.

As students practice thinking like Einstein, I walk around and listen in, complimenting, coaching, and giving feedback. I remind students to remember that even Einstein did not become genius overnight. With time and practice, students will become more skilled and confident questioners.

Lesson Four: Asking the Right Question at the Right Time

How often have you heard your students ask, So what's the right answer? I want students to learn to ask another kind of question: Do you think I have the right question? The ability to ask the right kind of question at the right time is the hallmark of a truly efficient and successful learner. Like drivers in a car, the right questions can plow the road ahead or leave us stuck in a ditch along the side of the highway. Being in charge of the questions we ask matters. Successful thinking and learning require questions to be framed in a wide variety of ways. The framing of our questions dramatically influences what we can and are able to understand. Just teaching students to question is not enough. It is critical to explore where different questions take them as learners.

The conversation that follows is how I help students become aware of using the right question at the right time.

> We have been talking a great deal lately about the importance of curiosity and asking powerful questions. I want to share with you a quote that I came across that will help us think about our work today as learners.
>
> Einstein once remarked that if he were about to be killed and had only one hour to figure out how to save his life, he would devote the first fifty-five minutes of that hour to searching for the right question. Once he had that question, Einstein said finding the answer would take only about five minutes.
>
> As learners, when we get to the point where we know what kind of question to ask, we are in a much better position to understand what we are reading and learning about. I want to share with you how different questions get us to different places. An "I wonder" question leads us in a different direction than a "How is it like" question. It is important for us to know how the types of questions we ask impact and influence the answers we are capable of getting.
>
> Over the next weeks, we are going to explore many kinds or types of questions together. These are the question types we'll be working with:
>
> - Clarifying questions
> - Sorting and sifting questions
> - Strategic questions
> - Planning questions
> - Elaboration questions
> - Comparing questions

These questions are based on the work of McKenzie (2005). I want students to see that each type of question is a tool in their thinking toolbox. A variety of tools may be needed to complete a project, and those tools must be chosen carefully. Forming questions is a challenge for many students who have never thought consciously about how they think or question. Thinking tools lie unsorted, unlabeled, and unidentifiable in the bottom of their box. They tend to reach into the box and pull out the first tool (or question) that comes to hand (or mind). This leads to hammering when drilling is needed instead.

To introduce students to the idea of categorizing questions, I suggest bringing in question tools. I talk to students about how the questions might be organized based on what they do. I help them recognize that questions can do many things: provide clarification, define sequence, categorize details, or make comparisons. This same sorting and labeling process can be used to explore questions we ask in reading and learning. Before long, students are able to reach into their questioning toolbox and consciously select the kind of question needed to reveal, reflect on, or respond to meaning. Types of questions are shown in table 3.1.

Table 3.1: Question Typology

Question Type	Examples
Essential Questions	What does it mean to be a digital citizen? What makes a good friend? How can we achieve true happiness? What is powerful community?
Elaborating Questions	What does this mean? What might it mean if . . .? How could I take this farther? What is missing? What has not been addressed?
Clarification Questions	What is the problem? How is this like . . .? Does this *really* mean . . .? Where did they gather the data? How was this verified? How can we verify . . .?
Hypothetical Questions	What if . . .? What if we were to . . .? Do you suppose that . . .? Could it be . . .?
Strategic Questions	How do I make sense of . . .? How does this fit? What tools and strategies will help me? What needs to be eliminated, reversed, or modified in order to make better sense of my findings?
Probing Questions	Which ideas are worth keeping? How is this new information changing my perspective? What have I not yet asked? What is still missing?
Planning Questions	How can I best approach this next step? The next challenge? What has already been done? What worked? Did not work? What can I try next? Who can help verify or support . . .?

continued→

Question Type	Examples
Unanswerable Questions	How will this matter?
	How will I be remembered?
	How will life be different when/if . . .?
	I wonder if we will ever know . . .
Provocative Questions	What's the point?
	Who cares?
	Will anyone listen?
	Who will hear me?

Visit **go.solution-tree.com/instruction** to download the handout *Question Typology*.

All questions differ in their power. The goal of this lesson is to enable students to experience the dynamic power of active, strategic questioning. The purpose is not to ensure that students can select and match the correct label to the kind of question they are asking. Questioning typology is a tool that helps students become aware of ways to frame their questions to serve their learning purposes. The question groups represent a continuum of increasing fluidity, dynamism, and strategic power. As students use questions from the various groups, they become more proficient learners. These experiences enable them to distinguish between the essential questions that pursue big themes and universal truths, and clarification questions that focus and monitor meaning.

Developing effective questioning strategies is integral to instruction in all areas of the curriculum. Nonetheless, many teachers find it helpful to plan a unit of study about question strategies. Suggestions for such a unit follow.

You might consider beginning with an essential question: one that is broad in scope and timeless in nature. Examples of essential questions are:

- What is justice?
- Is art a matter of talent or taste?
- How far should science go in the pursuit of preserving human life?
- Is war necessary?
- Does technology advance our society?

Faced with an authentic problem, students begin with asking questions about the topic being studied. Questions that guide students through inquiry are:

- What do I already know?
- What questions do I have?
- How do I find out?
- What did I learn?

These questions, gleaned from the students' natural curiosity, guide the research process leading students to find information from which they create their own knowledge and understanding about the topic. When students find answers to their own questions, their motivation and ownership are increased. Instructors act as coaches, guides, and facilitators, enabling learners to arrive at their true questions about things they really care about.

Probing and clarification questions help us gain the facts, details, and points of view necessary to pursue the answers to our essential questions. These questions help frame the multiple aspects of the discussion:

- What does that mean?
- What could that mean?
- What do you think about . . . ?
- What are the reasons for . . .?
- What is the relationship of . . . to . . . ?
- How has this issue impacted you? The community? The world?
- Where do you stand on . . . ?

As students delve more deeply into a topic, strategic and planning questions can help guide their thinking. These questions foster critical thinking:

- Is this known? How is this known?
- Which is the most important? Is this more important than . . . ?
- How do these compare? How do these contrast?
- What are the facts to support it?
- Where are the data? Where is the proof?

It is easy for learners to get overwhelmed with questions. However, the benefits of learning what to ask and how to frame the questions are immeasurable.

Student Habitude Reflection

Students can respond to these prompts for reflection on curiosity in their habitude notebooks.

My Reflections on Curiosity

Asking interesting questions helped me to learn . . .

Being curious helps me learn . . .

I am most curious to learn about . . .

The people I know who ask the most powerful questions are . . .

continued→

The questions I have found most useful when . . . are . . .

When I was asked a question in class today, I stopped and thought about . . . before answering.

I know I am becoming better at asking questions because . . .

Visit **go.solution-tree.com/instruction** to download the handout *My Reflections on Curiosity*.

Chapter Takeaway

By the end of the habitude study of curiosity, here are four things I want students to take away from our conversations:

1. Know that you should be courageous with questions. Lots of people saw apples fall, but only Sir Isaac Newton dared ask how or why. Someone smarter than I once said, "Ask the question, play the fool; don't ask the question, stay the fool." The only dumb question is the one not asked.

2. Know that questions help you. Questions allow us to make sense of the world. They are the most powerful tools we have for making decisions and solving problems, for inventing, changing, and improving our lives as well as the lives of others. Questioning is central to learning and growing.

3. Know that being curious brings fun and enjoyment. Happy people ask lots of questions. We grew up thinking that curiosity killed the cat. On the contrary, it was curiosity that gave the cat nine lives. Curious learners are happy learners. It is easy to find life fascinating and to begin wondering *why* and *how*.

4. Know that questions are important. Questions, not answers, define you as a learner. Celebrate when your students ask Why is the sky blue?, Who made clouds?, or What happens if . . . ? Let students know that their questions matter. The smartest students become the ones who ask the wisest questions.

Reflections

I think, at a child's birth, if a mother could ask a fairy godmother to endow it with the most useful gift, that gift would be curiosity.
—ELEANOR ROOSEVELT

Like parents holding a newborn infant, we can feel overwhelmed by the sense of responsibility for shaping young lives and minds. If our classrooms remain places where curiosity is nurtured, developed, and celebrated, the gift we give students extends far beyond the classroom walls.

We will be unable to give a gift we ourselves do not possess. The following questions are intended to help you model, demonstrate, and be more giving of your own curious learning life:

- In what ways are you curious?
- When was the last time you sought knowledge simply for the pursuit of it?
- How has curiosity enriched your life?
- What is the role of curiosity in your classroom?
- In what ways are your students curious?
- When is the last time your students were allowed to seek knowledge in a topic they were curious about?
- What have you done in your classroom environment to enrich and support curiosity development?

Curiosity Resources for Students

Banyai, I. (1998). *Zoom*. New York: Puffin Books.

Banyai, I. (1998). *ReZoom*. New York: Puffin Books.

Curtis, J. C. (2000). *Where do balloons go? An uplifting mystery*. New York: HarperCollins.

Franson, S. E. (2007). *Un-Brella*. New York: Roaring Brook Press.

Gutierrez, E. (2007). *Picturescape*. Vancouver, BC: Simply Read Books.

Knauer, K. (2006). *Exploring the unexplained: The world's greatest marvels, mysteries and myths*. New York: Time Books.

McCloskey, R. (1989). *A time of wonder*. New York: Puffin Books.

Merriam, E. (1999). *The wise woman and her secret*. New York: Aladdin.

Muth, J. (2002). *The three questions*. New York: Scholastic.

Rey, H. A. (2010). *The complete adventures of Curious George: 70th anniversary edition*. Boston: HMH Books.

Rylant, C. (1983). *Miss Maggie*. New York: Dutton.

Seeger, L. V. (2010). *The hidden alphabet*. New York: Roaring Book Press.

Silverstein, S. (1981). *The light in the attic*. New York: HarperCollins.

Van Allsburg, C. (1984). *The mysteries of Harris Burdick*. New York: Houghton Mifflin.

Van Allsburg, C. (1986). *The stranger*. New York: Houghton Mifflin.

Van Allsburg, C. (1988). *Two bad ants*. New York: Houghton Mifflin.

Wiesner, D. (1999). *Sector 7*. New York: Clarion Books

Wollard, K., & Solomon, D. (1993). *How come? Every kid's science questions explained*. New York: Workman.

Curiosity Resources for Teachers

Barell, J. (2003). *Developing more curious minds.* Alexandria, VA: Association for Supervision and Curriculum Development.

Harvey, S., & Goudvis, A. (2007). *Strategies that work: Teaching comprehension for understanding and engagement*. Portland, ME: Stenhouse.

Koechlin, C., & Zwaan, S. (1997). *Teaching tools for the information age*. Markham, ON: Pembroke.

Koechlin, C., & Zwaan, S. (2001). *Info tasks for successful learning*: *Building skills in reading, writing, and research*. Portland, ME: Stenhouse.

Koechlin, C., & Zwaan, S. (2005). *Build your own information literate school*. Santa Barbara, CA: Libraries Unlimited.

McKenzie, J. (2005). *Learning to question to wonder to learn*. Bellingham, WA: FNO Press.

Morgan, N., & Saxton, J. (2006). *Asking better questions* (2nd ed.). Markham, ON: Pembroke.

CHAPTER 4
Self-Awareness

*Knowing others is wisdom, knowing
yourself is enlightenment.*

— LAO TZU

As lifelong learners, our growth should never cease. Part of our growth is improving our understanding of self—why we feel what we feel, how we behave, and why we behave. This understanding affords us opportunity and independence in changing ourselves, allowing us to create the life we desire. Yet without fully knowing ourselves—who we are, what we believe, why we make certain choices—self-acceptance and change are all the more difficult. Let's review the definition of the habitude of self-awareness:

> Self-awareness provides a system of checks and balances that equips individuals to understand themselves and to make conscious choices and deliberate decisions about the direction and quality of their lives.

The quest for self-knowledge goes beyond articulating what we want from life or who we want to become. Self-awareness is the ability to simultaneously exist both inside and outside of ourselves. With this intimate knowledge, we're able to recognize our strengths and limitations and use that awareness proactively as well as retrospectively. Self-awareness can act as an advance alert system when there are conflicts that exist between our true nature and what we are actually doing or thinking. We may not always know how to reach our destination, and may from time to time become lost, but at the very least, we'll understand when we're off track and be able to search mindfully for a new route.

Helping our students recognize how self-awareness can both guide and empower is what makes this a habitude worth the study.

The Pitch: Why Self-Awareness Matters

Knowing who you are, where you are going, and what you want to be when you grow up are obvious benefits in your life's quest. But how does self-awareness pertain to learning? Is the quest to know yourself as a learner equally beneficial? The answer is unequivocally yes. As I introduce the idea of self-awareness in relation to learning to students, I focus on what champion learners do.

> ## Champion Learners
> - Recognize their strengths and weaknesses, making them more able to match their abilities to specific situations and settings
> - Are self-driven, set goals, make plans, and learn with purpose and passion
> - Monitor their behaviors, actions, and thinking to ensure they are staying on track toward their goals
> - Are more confident and successful—they know what they are doing and what it takes to get there
> - Are efficient and able to make clear decisions about the best way to apply strategies and techniques to further their goals

Far too often, students see learning as something done to them. They look for solutions to their challenges outside of themselves—in teachers, in books, in classmates. Students leave our classrooms with answers about a lot of stuff but with too many questions about themselves:

- How will I handle a challenge?
- Do I have the strategies it takes?
- What gifts do I bring to the world?
- Can my gifts help me engage in the world?

The conversations in the following lessons are intended to help students become experts about themselves so they learn how to make the best use of their abilities, skills, and talents. Combined with smart teaching, this situation becomes a win-win for all!

The Anchor: The Million-Dollar Conversation Starter

The conversation I have with students includes reflection questions that can be used to create individual learner profiles:

> *When I talk to you about learning, many times our conversations are about what we are learning or what I want you to know or do. Today's conversation is all about you and who you are as learners. This is a conversation about the habitude of self-awareness. Successful learning involves more than just knowledge of the content—it involves knowledge of yourself as a learner.*

Self-aware learners know how they learn best. They are able to recognize their strengths and weaknesses, and most importantly are able to monitor and control their own learning process. In this way, your learning success is not up to someone else; it is something I want you to be in charge of for yourself. It is what I want most for you, to feel confident and in charge of your own learning. Becoming self-aware is the first step to getting you there. So let's get to know ourselves, shall we?

I want to be clear. There is no right or wrong way to learn. Just like finger-prints, every learner is different and therefore has different needs to make learning successful. Some learners work better by themselves in a quiet room; others need people around to keep them focused and motivated. Each and every one of you has a unique learner personality. You each have different strengths, different challenges. The goal of our lesson today is for you to recognize what your strengths and challenges are so you can figure out how you work and learn best.

Here's what I would like you to do. Close your eyes and think about a learning experience that was very positive for you—one you learned a lot from or were successful in doing. It can be anything from tying your shoes to learning how to swim. It doesn't have to be learning that happened in school. After the image is clear in your mind, take a few minutes and draw or sketch what is happening. Jot down some words or ideas that come to mind about the experience. As we share, I am going to ask you some questions to help you pinpoint specific things that are important to you as a learner.

I use the following questions to excavate the specific conditions and characteristics of students' learning styles and preferences. These questions can be easily adapted across grade levels and content areas.

- *What did you learn most recently?*
- *Why did you want to learn this? What was your purpose for learning?*
- *Was your learning motivated by curiosity or necessity?*
- *How did the learning happen—by doing, watching, talking, or studying?*
- *Who else was involved in the learning process? How did they help or hinder?*
- *Where did the learning take place? Did you like that place?*
- *How did you know you were successful?*
- *Would you have liked anything to go differently?*

(Visit **go.solution-tree.com/instruction** to download the handout *Learning Styles and Preferences*.)

I repeat this process the second day, but this time I ask the students to reflect on an unsuccessful or difficult learning experience.

At the culmination of the conversations, I have the students share their reflections and discoveries. Then I give them the task of creating a learner profile that begins with these two statements:

1. I am the sort of person who learns well when . . .

2. I am the sort of person who does not learn well when . . .

The learner profile can be expanded and entered into a learning portfolio. A learning portfolio is an easy-to-manage practical tool that provides students with a place to record their goals and reflect on themselves as learners. Even young students are capable of setting learning goals and charting their accomplishments. When students are encouraged to compile artifacts and record their progress during the year, they are able to take ownership of their learning.

The learning portfolio can include a number of items:

1. A learner profile based on questions designed to explore students' learning conditions and characteristics (see page 58–59)

2. A strengths assessment that provides answers to these questions:

    + Who are you as a reader/learner?

    + Can you describe your learning style?

    + What do you see yourself accomplishing in the next five years, ten years . . . ?

    + What steps have you taken toward attaining that success?

    + How does feedback or messages from others impact your learning?

    + What are your strengths?

    (Visit **go.solution-tree.com/instruction** to download the handout *Who Am I as a Learner?*)

3. A goal sheet that describes what students can do to maximize strengths and which strategies students can use to overcome weaknesses

4. Samples of reading and writing work that reflect the application of the strategies students are working on

5. Self-selected items that students have chosen to highlight something they have worked hard to accomplish

6. Samples that provide evidence of reading and thinking strategies that have successfully transferred to other subjects—for example, a math or science journal

Learning portfolios are valuable resources you can use to observe students' development over time. During individual conferences, students can use items from the portfolio to explain what they are accomplishing and to specify where they need additional guidance. You can enhance your students' use of their portfolios through observations about the contents and what they reveal about the students' skills and abilities.

For learners to become self-aware, and ultimately more effective, these beginning conversations are critical. With knowledge of their learning strengths and preferences, students are well on their way to being the independent, thoughtful, and self-directed learners we desire.

Conversations That Last: Continuing the Dialogue

Self-awareness cannot be mastered. It develops over time and with practice. The following lessons provide you with specific ideas and tools to build self-awareness within your students. These lessons do not follow a prescribed scope and sequence. They can and should be expanded and extended over days and weeks. These conversations keep the habitude alive and moving, enabling students to link self-awareness to their work at school and to their lives. Before embarking on additional lessons about self-awareness, you may find it useful to have your students complete a self-awareness inventory that features these topics:

- My best trait is . . .
- I struggle most with . . .
- My favorite learning environment is . . .
- I help myself most by . . .
- Something that gets in the way of my learning is . . .
- I learn best by . . .
- I am interested in . . .
- My goals are . . .

Visit **go.solution-tree.com/instruction** to download the handout *Self-Awareness Inventory*.

Lesson One: The Story of Me

The stories we tell not only give others information about our lives—who we are, what we do, and why we do it—but also enable us to reflect on our behaviors and what they mean. It is important to give students the opportunity to discover themselves by exploring their personal story.

The best stories come straight from the heart. My favorite strategy for helping students find the way to their hearts and tell their story is called *heart mapping*, based on the work of Georgia Heard (1998). Here is an example of the conversation I have with students:

One of the best ways we can get to know one another is through our story. Great writers and storytellers speak from their hearts. In order to do that, we have to do some work first to know what's in our hearts, to know what we really care about and what's really important about our lives that we want to share with others. Georgia Heard is a writer who describes the process of getting to know your heart in her book Awakening the Heart.

We are going to use a technique that Heard calls heart mapping. It is one that poets, writers, storytellers, and leaders use. Your heart map is a representation of all the important things that are in your heart, all the things that matter to you. The map can include anything that has stayed in your heart because you care a lot about it—people and places you care about, moments and memories that have stayed with you, or things you love to do.

Let's think about some questions to get us started on creating our heart maps:

- *What has really affected your heart?*
- *What people have been important to you?*
- *What are some experiences or central events that you will never forget?*
- *What happy or sad memories do you have?*
- *What secrets have you kept in your heart?*
- *What small or big things are important to you?*

As students display and share who they are and what they are most passionate about, I use these additional questions to help them explore the ideas further and take the conversation even deeper:

- *Should some things be outside the heart and others inside?*
- *Do you want to draw more than one heart? Happy or sad? Secret or open?*
- *What's at the center of your heart? What occupies the outer edges?*
- *Do different colors represent different emotions, events, or relationships?*
- *Are there parts of your heart you are willing to share with others? Parts you want to keep private? How will you represent both?*

How we see ourselves inside determines how and why we do our work with and around others. It is the work of knowing ourselves from the inside out that allows us to work successfully on the outside. Heart maps are a wonderful way to sharpen that inner vision.

The students' participation in this activity may vary. Sometimes I'll record students' contributions on chart paper or a whiteboard. Other times, I let the conversation flow without providing any written support. Alternatively, I sometimes conclude the lesson by having students record their heart maps in their habitude notebooks. I encourage them to review their heart maps periodically to add new ideas that show their growth in self-awareness. In Lesson Two you will find more suggestions for helping students expand their heart maps.

For examples of heart-mapping activities with students, you might be interested in viewing many examples of heart designs that students can adapt for their heart-mapping activities; try searching Google for heart-mapping images.

Lesson Two: What Makes Me, Me?

Following up on the conversations from Lesson One, I introduce this question: what makes me, me? Over the next days and weeks, I have students select one or more of the following questions to respond to in their habitudes notebooks:

1. How do I describe me?

2. What causes me to smile, laugh, or get excited?

3. What captures my attention, gets me interested, or makes me want to stay longer at a task or an event?

4. What do I always seem to make time for?

5. What occupies my mind even when I do not have time to do it? What do I think about most?

6. What do people notice most about me?

7. When people meet me for the first time, what is the most common thing they say?

8. What words do others use to describe me?

9. What words do I use to describe myself?

10. When I am alone, I almost always . . .

11. When I am with my friends, we most like to . . .

12. How am I different than my friends?

13. What makes me unique?

14. What makes me most happy?

15. Now use your answers to those questions to help you answer this one: what makes me, me?

Visit **go.solution-tree.com/instruction** to download the handout *What Makes Me, Me?*

Students can respond in any way to these prompts—writing, illustrating, or reflecting. I make clear to students that the goal is self-awareness and expression. There are no right or wrong answers—only discoveries!

Lesson Three: My One Special Thing!

In this lesson, I have students work with partners to explore further what makes individuals unique. This lesson expands on the approach used in Lesson Two, in which students were determining how to answer the question, What makes me, me? The conversation with students and the activity I have them complete follows.

> Putting into words who we are and what makes us special is sometimes hard to do. It is important to find friends and mentors who will help us in the process of self-discovery. Today, we are going to work with partners, helping one another reflect on the unique and special aspects of our lives and stories.

> The questions your partner will be asking you are intended to help you discover the things that make you stand out and special. Knowing your talents, passions, and gifts will help you know what to work on as a learner and friend, but also will help you work as a more productive community citizen because you will know exactly what you have to contribute to the world.

> Remember, some of our best talents are hidden. Let your partner help you uncover exactly what those talents are.

The following questions can be used to guide and focus the students' interviews with each other. I discuss each question with the students using the examples to help them broaden their thinking about themselves as they interview one another. Comments and examples I discuss with the students accompany each question.

1. **Your knowledge:** What do you know a lot about?

   Your knowledge may be about anything and can come from any source. It could be about animals, sports, musical instruments, history, building or creating something, surviving a difficult time, handling a sickness or disease, secrets to being healthy or happy, or making others happy.

2. **Your skills:** What do you know how to do well?

   These may include skills developed and used at school, around the house, in sports or games, with hobbies, in recreational activities, or in anything else that you do. They could be training, experiments, competing or being a competitor, reading well, studying, new technology, video games, taking care of someone, or something else.

3. **Your strengths:** What is the characteristic you are most known for?

   When people describe you, what do they say you are good at? They could mention things like: very disciplined, always positive and happy, always makes people feel good or happy, careful, trustworthy, or not afraid to speak up.

4. **Your abilities:** What kinds of things do you believe you have a talent for?

   These may include having the ability to organize things, having the ability to get my friends and family motivated, or being good at fixing things.

5. **Your interests:** What kinds of things do you *love* to do?

   What have you dreamed of doing if you had the chance? What have you not tried but would like to? What do you like to do in your free time?

6. **Your experience:** What are some interesting things you have done and seen in your life?

   Our personal experiences not only shape what we know, they can shape who we are and may become. Even if the experiences we have may be ones that we do not wish to repeat, every experience is an important learning tool. Think about what you have experienced that could be used to help you in this new project. What experiences were the most exciting? Difficult? Remarkable? What have you done that you might want build on?

   For instance, I traveled to another country, I met someone who . . . , I played the piano for five years, I was a part of a club, I tried something scary, I learned to . . . , or I volunteered.

7. Your one special thing!

   This interview was a treasure map leading us to uncover all your hidden talents. What is the one special thing that stands out now?

Visit **go.solution-tree.com/instruction** to download the handout *My One Special Thing!*

Lesson Four: We Have a Problem

Houston, we have a problem is a catchy expression students can use to indicate they need help. The inner commands or voices we hear as we read have the power to both engage and distract (Tovani, 2000). Students need to become aware that it is critically important to be in control of their reading processes. You can remind them that even champion readers engage in inner conversations that sometimes lead them to stray far from the meaning. It is important for students to realize that our minds can lapse into daydreaming or dwell on personal issues that intrude. If the reader finds a subject uninteresting or an author boring, the potential for intrusive and distracting thoughts is especially high. Readers may also become waylaid by struggles with difficult language or challenging ideas.

A think-aloud procedure is an effective way to model the effects of engaging and distracting voices while reading. I like to model these behaviors using *Now One Foot, Now the Other* (dePaola, 2006). My conversation follows.

> *As I read, there is silent conversation going on. In my head, I hear a voice reading the words. It lets me know if I am reciting the words accurately and that they sound like I am talking aloud and not robotic. But another voice I am*

aware of and attend to is the voice that talks to and interacts with the writer. This is the voice that helps me understand the words I hear myself reciting. I call that my conversation voice, because it is like I am having the conversation with the author as if we were sitting together in my room. Thinking about the writer in this way helps me interact with the ideas in the book.

Let me tell you about what happened when I was reading a book by one of my favorite authors.

Last night, I was reading Now One Foot, Now the Other *by Tomie dePaola, one of my favorite authors. In the story, the main character has a relative who gets sick. My conversation voice was sad because I thought about the time I found out my grandfather had just had a stroke. I remembered those feelings and found it very easy to connect to the character, Bobby, as he was wrestling with those same worries. Along with these thoughts came my memory pictures of my grandfather and me as we played games, sang funny songs, and went on special trips together. Then I started to wonder if Tomie dePaola had experienced illness with someone in his family, as I know authors sometimes write about things in their own lives. Even days later, the ideas in the text were still with me. When I'm talking back to the text and getting pictures in my mind, I remember more, and I understand more.*

I ask students to describe times when they have heard their conversation or interacting voice as they read. I ask them to explain what their conversation with the author was like. As students share their experiences, they become aware of the different ways in which individuals respond to what they read.

I also want students to recognize that the conversation voice isn't always a good thing. My goal for the second session is to model how the conversation voice can sometimes lead a reader astray with thoughts that distract from the author's message. Again, I referenced *Now One Foot, Now the Other* (dePaola, 2006):

As I read about Bobby and his grandfather watching the fireworks, I started to remember the first time I took my kids to see fireworks. My daughter Abby was really scared—she jumped every time there was a pop.

Did you catch how my mind started to wander? That was my distracting voice.

I explain to students that connections to the text are very important to help understand and remember what you are reading, but you have to be careful with them. Sometimes one thought will lead to another, and before you know it, you're thinking about something else. That's the distracting voice in action—the one that leads you away from the text.

Over the next several sessions with students, I brainstorm ways to reel in the distracting voice and re-engage with the text. Together we explore strategies that Tovani (2000; 2004) has used to enable her adolescent students to become more proficient readers. These strategies include:

- Reading slower

- Re-reading
- Pausing and asking a question
- Creating a picture in your mind

How about you? How do you re-engage with the text? Share your strategies and techniques with students often.

Student Habitude Reflection

Students can respond to these prompts for reflection on self-awareness in their habitude notebooks.

My Reflections on Self-Awareness

My greatest strengths as a learner are . . .

These are the strengths that I have learned by . . .

When I evaluated my learning today, I found that . . .

When I am successful in my learning, I feel . . .

What frustrates me most about my learning is . . .

I am aware of how others describe me as a learner . . .

These are the things that I need to take more care doing . . .

I was able to correct myself today when . . .

Visit **go.solution-tree.com/instruction** to download the handout *My Reflections on Self-Awareness*.

Chapter Takeaway

Successful learning is not about getting things done, but rather knowing how you got it done, so that you can do it again later and better.

The two questions I want students wondering about everyday as they leave their habitude lessons are:

1. What did I learn about myself as a reader, a writer, and a learner today?

2. What did I learn that I can do again and again and again?

Reflections

We shower children with awards and recognition because we hope to build confidence. This reinforcement is external and temporary. Confidence comes from within. It is a byproduct of self-awareness, a result of knowing our strengths and weaknesses. Self-awareness comes from success and failure, independently achieved. There are no awards for self-awareness, but it engenders strength of character. How much better it is to nurture self-awareness in children than to fill their cabinets with awards and trophies.

To help students better understand themselves, we can be the model of how self-awareness has influenced our actions and behaviors. To be an effective model, you need to be aware of your own attributes as a learner. If you haven't already done so, refer to the handouts *What Makes Me, Me?* and *My One Special Thing!* to guide your reflections (visit **go.solution-tree.com/instruction** for these handouts). Think about what you discover about yourself as you answer the questions. How can you use what you know about yourself as a learner to help your students become more effective learners?

Self-Awareness Resources for Students

Adler, D. (2005). *America's champion swimmer: Gertrude Ederle*. Mooloolaba, Australia: Sandpiper.

Aesop. (1984). *Tortoise and the hare: An Aesop fable*. New York: Holiday House.

Aldis, D. (1978). *Nothing is impossible*. Gloucester, MA: Smith.

Bennett, W. (1996). *The book of virtues*. New York: Simon & Schuster.

Bradby, M. (1995). *More than anything else*. London: Orchard Books.

Brown, M. (1991). *D. W. Flips*. New York: Little, Brown.

Buck, P. S. (1986). *The big wave*. New York: HarperCollins.

Bunting, E. (1990). *How many days to America?* Mooloolaba, Australia: Sandpiper.

Cameron, P. *"I can't" said the ant*. New York: Scholastic.

Climo, S. (1999). *The little red ant and the great big crumb*. Mooloolaba, Australia: Sandpiper.

Coerr, E. (2004). *Sadako and the thousand paper cranes*. New York: Puffin Books.

dePaola, T. (1978). *Pancakes for breakfast*. Mooloolaba, Australia: Sandpiper.

Frank, A. (1953). *The diary of a young girl*. New York: Pocket Books.

Galdone , P. (2011). *The little red hen*. Boston: Houghton Mifflin Harcourt.

Gardiner, J. R. (1997). *Stone fox*. New York: Houghton Mifflin.

George, J. C. (2003). *Julie of the wolves*. New York: HarperTeen.

Krauss, R. (2004). *Carrot seed*. Pine Plains, NY: Live Oak Media.

Krull, K. (2000). *Wilma unlimited: How Wilma Rudolph became the world's fastest woman*. Mooloolaba, Australia: Sandpiper.

Lester, J. (1999). *John Henry*. New York: Puffin Books.

MacLachlan, P. (2004). *Sarah plain and tall*. New York: HarperCollins.

Martin, J. B. (2009). *Snowflake Bentley*. Mooloolaba, Australia: Sandpiper.

McCully, A. (1997). *Mirette on the high wire*. New York: Puffin Books.

O'Dell, S. (2010). *Island of the blue dolphins*. Mooloolaba, Australia: Sandpiper.

Olsen, J. (1974). *Jackie Robinson: Pro ball's first Black star*. Mankato, MN: Creative Education.

Paterson, K. (1987). *The great Gilly Hopkins*. New York: HarperCollins.

Paulsen, G. (2000). *Hatchet*. New York: Scholastic.

Piper, W. (2005). *The little engine that could*. New York: Philomel Books.

Pippen, S. (1997). *Scottie Pippen: Reach higher*. Taylor Trade.

Sachar, L. (2008). *Holes*. New York: Farrar, Straus & Giroux.

Sachs, M. (2005). *Veronica Ganz*. New York: The Authors Guild.

Sachs, M. (2007). *Lost in America*. New York: Roaring Book Press.

Sperry, A. (2008). *Call it courage*. New York: Simon Pulse.

Szabo, C. (2007). *Sky pioneer: A photobiography of Amelia Earhart*. Des Moines, IA: National Geographic.

Viorst, J. (2009). *Alexander and the terrible, horrible, no good, very bad day*. New York: Atheneum Books.

Williams, V. B. (1984). *A chair for my mother*. New York: Greenwillow Books.

Winston, R. (2010). *What makes me me?* New York: Dorling Kindersley Books.

Woods, E. (2006). *Start something: You can make a difference*. New York: Simon & Schuster.

Yolen, J. (1999). *Wizards hall*. Mooloolaba, Australia: Sandpiper.

Self-Awareness Resources for Teachers

Allen, R. E., & Allen, S. D. (1997). *Winnie-the-Pooh on success: In which you, Pooh, and friends learn about the most important subject of all*. New York: Penguin.

Bryk, A. S., & Schneider, B. (2002). *Trust in schools: A core resource for improvement*. New York: Russell Sage Foundation.

Courtenay, B. (1996). *The power of one*. New York: Ballantine Books.

Covey, S. R. (1989). *The 7 habits of highly effective people: Restoring the character ethic*. New York: Simon & Schuster.

Delpit, L. (2006). *Other people's children: Cultural conflict in the classroom*. New York: New Press.

Finkelstein, S. (2003). *Why smart executives fail: And what you can learn from their mistakes*. New York: Portfolio.

Jackson, R. R. (2009). *Never work harder than your students & other principles of great teaching*. Alexandria, VA: Association for Supervision and Curriculum Development.

Kobrin, D. (2004). *In there with the kids: Creating lessons that connect with students* (2nd ed.). Alexandria, VA: Association for Supervision and Curriculum Development.

Moss, W. L. (2004). *Children don't come with an instruction manual: A teacher's guide to problems that affect learners*. New York: Teachers College Press.

Noer, D. M. (1997). *Breaking free: A prescription for personal and organizational change*. San Francisco: Jossey-Bass.

O'Faolain, N. (1996). *Are you somebody? The accidental memoir of a Dublin woman*. New York: Holt.

Zmuda, A. (2010). *Breaking free from the myths about teaching and learning: Innovation as an engine for student success*. Alexandria, VA: Association for Supervision and Curriculum Development.

CHAPTER 5

Perseverance

Nobody trips over mountains. It is the small pebble that causes you to stumble. Pass all the pebbles in your path and you will find you have crossed the mountain.

— AUTHOR UNKNOWN

Recently, I cleared a mountain. I completed running in my first half-marathon. Physically and mentally, the critical aspects of perseverance came to life. Just one year prior, I had never run a mile, let alone completed a marathon. It was just too big a mountain. As our training team reflected on this experience, we agreed our turning point came when we stopped trying to climb the mountain (run the marathon) and began concentrating on the pebbles—our day-to-day commitment to running. Once we knew we could endure rain, snow, lack of sleep, and apathy, we realized we were champions before we stepped one foot into the race. We lived the habitude of perseverance. It was this experience that helped me unpack what I think I've always known but rarely articulated about perseverance. Success is not always about the mountains we climb but rather our ability to handle the pebbles in our pathway. Our *running stories*, those stories of perseverance, should be shared in every classroom.

Let's review the definition of the habitude of perseverance:

> Perseverance is the ability to sustain interest, effort, and commitment in any circumstance that life presents.

Persevering is not an easy task for many of us, and for our students it may be even more challenging. Think about your students and the opportunities they have at school or in their homes and communities to witness perseverance in action. What examples of perseverance do they encounter in the worlds of entertainment and sports? Where are the positive role models that will enable your students to recognize what it means to persevere? Developing the habitude of perseverance requires patience and self-awareness, especially when things are not going as smoothly as one might wish. As you work with your students on this habitude, you may find that on occasion your ability to persevere is tested. But doesn't that happen with lots of things we encounter as teachers?

The Pitch: Why Perseverance Matters

Perseverance is the cornerstone of any successful endeavor, in school and out. It is a key to victory over unfavorable circumstances. It is also the source of excellence that can impel students to be successful learners. A student's commitment to excellence requires the ability to:

- Set clearly defined goals
- Show the courage of one's convictions
- Manage one's actions and reactions to unexpected circumstances
- Dream big with passion fueling the way

The following lessons and conversations will help students build their perseverance muscles as they train like intellectual athletes.

The Anchor: The Million-Dollar Conversation Starter

What is perseverance? How do I recognize it? Do I have it? My goal for this first conversation with the students is to answer these questions. Here's how we start.

I place a wrapped toy, preferably one that is difficult to open, in front of the group. The more the packaging is like Fort Knox, the better. I make sure to select an item that is appropriate to the grade level in both enticement and difficulty— I often use toys. I give the students adequate time to struggle opening the package. After they get the package open or give up on the task, I draw their attention to what I am going to write on the board. I turn to the board and write this definition:

> Perseverance—The act of continuing to do something in spite of difficulty or opposition.

As we reflect on this experience, I have students discuss the following:

- *What kept you from throwing the toy across the room when you got frustrated?*
- *What were you saying to yourself? What made you keep you trying?*
- *How did others help? How did they hinder?*

From our experiment of opening a well-sealed object, students recognize that someone has persevered when they observe evidence of:

- Commitment, hard work, patience, and endurance
- Ability to handle difficulty calmly and without complaint
- Use of alternative means to accomplish the task
- Acceptance of support and encouragement within one's self or others

Following the discussion of how to recognize perseverance, I like to bring in some timeless stories that provide examples of these principles in action. I often use *The Little Engine That Could* (Piper, 2005) for this activity. This simple story illustrates how optimism and perseverance combine to achieve success.

I want students to see how perseverance affects their lives. To do so, I have them work together in small groups to discuss specific examples of how they demonstrated perseverance in our toy experience. Each group provides a quick summary of the discussion. Then, I move the discussion into the students' learning lives by providing examples of when these habits are present in the classroom. I explain to the students that they show me perseverance when they:

- Give up TV time to spend hours studying
- Keep trying to complete a new assignment that is difficult
- Continue to study even when discouraged by a problem
- Come to school after a hard night and still try to do their best
- Work hard to catch up after missing a day of school
- Cross the finish line even though the race is difficult
- Try out for something again, even if they weren't successful the first time

A great follow-up to this discussion is the book *I Knew You Could* (Dorfman, 2003). I want students to know they have persevered in some way, and they can and must continue to do so in order to be successful. For deeper reflection, I have students complete these two sentences in their habitudes notebook:

1. I show perseverance when . . .
2. I know it because I . . .

Conversations That Last: Continuing the Dialogue

Perseverance cannot be mastered. It develops over time and with practice. The following perseverance lessons provide you with specific ideas and tools to build students' understanding of this habitude. These lessons do not follow a prescribed scope and sequence. They can and should be expanded and extended over days and weeks. These conversations keep the habitude alive and moving, enabling students to link perseverance to their work at school and to their lives.

Lesson One: What You Do Makes You!

We form our habits, and then our habits form us.
— ROB GILBERT

I use this quote to introduce students to the idea that our behaviors—what we do or don't do—can be indicators of who we are as individuals and how others perceive us. I usually develop this lesson in two sessions. The first session focuses on the positive aspects of behavior—what we do and the possible results. In the second session, I have the students address the less positive aspects—what we don't do and the possible results.

After I present the quote, I have this conversation with the students:

> *What Rob Gilbert is saying in this powerful quote is that the habits we adopt and create either can shape and improve our lives, or they can lead us farther away from our goals and dreams. If we want to improve our lives and learning, then we must be aware of and take responsibility for our daily behaviors, actions, and attitudes through which we approach our work and learning.*
>
> *Have you ever heard someone say that you are what you eat to illustrate the connection between what you eat and your overall health and wellness? In the same way that doctors and health professionals encourage you to be aware of the food choices you make, I want to encourage you to be aware of the behaviors you engage in every day.*
>
> *Successful learning is not simply a matter of knowing; it is the result of doing. It is important to be aware and in control of the behaviors that will give you the most powerful results and outcomes. So we are going to take some time to reflect on the things you are doing every day: your behaviors, routines, and habits and how they may or may not be contributing to your goals as a learner.*
>
> *At the top of a page in your habitudes notebook, write this heading in bold letters:* **YOU ARE WHAT YOU DO.**
>
> *Next, draw a line down the middle of a page. Make a list of the things you do every day or almost every day in the left column. Think about all the possible results that could be achieved if these behaviors became part of your learning habitudes. List those results in the right column.*

To ensure that students get off to a good start with this activity, I provide an example, as shown in table 5.1.

In the next phase of this lesson (which may continue in another class period), I again refer to Gilbert's quote and have students reflect on the flip side: what people *don't do* reveals who they are. I follow the same procedure having the students record ideas in their habitudes notebook.

> *At the top of a page in your habitudes notebook, write this heading in bold letters:* **WHAT YOU DON'T DO MAKES YOU, TOO!**

Table 5.1: What I Do and Possible Results

What I Do (Daily Behavior)	Possible Results (Examples)
Read for twenty minutes	I get to explore a lot more books. I find that I am getting more fluent. I have learned new vocabulary words.
Write down all my assignments in a notebook	I feel more organized. I don't miss deadlines. I get less stressed.
Take notes in class	I remember more. I study more efficiently.
Find a study partner	I feel more confident when I practice with others. I push myself more when I know someone else is counting on me.

Visit **go.solution-tree.com/instruction** to download the handout *What I Do and Possible Results*.

> We all have traits we like and those we don't. But we have a lot more control over our lives than we think we do. In this next assignment, I want you to make a list of the things you don't do in your day and consider the result of not doing that. This is a challenging test of yourself awareness. It is important that you are specific and honest with your reflection.

Similar to the procedure I used in the first part of this lesson, I may discuss examples as shown in table 5.2 to help students begin to reflect on their responses to this activity.

Table 5.2: What I Don't Do and Possible Results

What I Don't Do (Daily Behavior)	Possible Results (Examples)
Manage my time	I am always staying up the night before the assignment is due, wishing I would have been working on it sooner.
Go to bed early on school nights	I am always tired in class. This makes it hard to pay attention to what my teachers are saying. I know that I miss a lot of important things in the lessons.
Prepare in advance for tests	I wait until the last minute to study, and then when I go to study, there is so much to remember that I get very stressed.

Visit **go.solution-tree.com/instruction** to download the handout *What I Don't Do and Possible Results*.

I provide a realistic amount of time for students to record some ideas in their habitudes notebooks. Together we discuss the implications of things that we don't do.

> If you want to be even more proactive, ask your family about your habits. Or, do some research relating to your examples. Consider these questions:
>
> * How many hours do the best readers in your school spend in reading activities?
>
> * How do the smartest students you know study?
>
> * What behaviors do the best learners exhibit while they are in class? In the library? With friends? Alone studying?
>
> One way to improve your ability to persevere is to give yourself a challenge. So, here's your challenge:
>
> Choose one behavior to focus on for the rest of the month. It takes thirty days to undo a habit or build a new one. Set an appointment for when you will work on or do that habit. Read and study how others have accomplished great results from that habitude. Decide to put that habitude into your learning lifestyle. One small change in your daily behaviors and attitude can yield extraordinary results.

Lesson Two: Life Is What Happens

Perseverance is the ability to not only do what you are supposed to do and get done what needs to be done but also to continue the effort no matter what. I begin this lesson with an exploration of famous individuals and their success stories. As we look at some great historical figures, we find many of them persevered against tremendous odds. Though we admire their accomplishments, the focus of this conversation is the enduring qualities that allowed these individuals to find success in life.

> When I think of people who have achieved their goals while enduring incredible obstacles, I think of Abraham Lincoln overcoming the lack of formal education. I think of Gandhi and Martin Luther King Jr., who both overcame hatred and prejudice. Viktor Frankl was able to survive the brutality of Nazi concentration camps and the loss of all that was dear to him. The list can go on and on of incredible achievements of valor, glory, and fame. The point I really want to make is how perseverance is not a magical quality but a mindset—an attitude—of how we view the obstacles we face in life.
>
> Persevering through a task is easy to do when nothing gets in the way. But how often does that happen? The difficulty lies in the obstacles or challenges we face in developing a habitude. We all know that things get in the way and that life can be hard. Isn't that right? Real perseverance happens when you act in spite of opposition.

Let's look at some examples of people who persevered in the face of huge difficulties. Their ability to persevere led to triumph. For many people, sickness, disability, and adversity would have been nothing more than a tragedy. Each one of these individuals became better, not bitter, because of the circumstances.

People Who Persevered to Overcome Challenges

Beethoven (composer)—deaf

Ray Charles (musician)—blind

Thomas Edison (inventor)—learning problems

Albert Einstein (scientist)—learning disability

Helen Keller (author)—deaf and blind

Franklin D. Roosevelt (president)—paralyzed from polio

Vincent van Gogh (artist)—mentally ill

Christopher Reeve (actor)—paralyzed from an accident

I want students to understand that these remarkable people are examples of how to act when adversity or tragedy enters life.

Students can brainstorm ways they can behave in the face of adversity. Many responses can get personal, but it's important, in some way, to have them make their accomplishments public. I take note when I see students:

- Face and accept what happens to them
- Express and talk about the feelings they are having
- Get help and support of others
- Learn and grow from the experience, even when it hurts
- Try to make a situation better

I want students to understand that people aren't able to persevere because they are famous or successful, though their success and fame are due in large part to their ability to persevere. People persevere because they make deliberate choices about what they will or will not do.

Lesson Three: Failure Leads to Success

Persevering learners view failure as a learning experience, using each mistake as tuition and each situation as an opportunity to glean something new. Stories of individuals overcoming the odds are an inspiration to all, but a very small percentage of people actually achieve their full potential because they give up after the first sign of struggle. The phrase *try, try again* is not just fodder for encouragement but is a clarion call that some people ignore, which causes them to fail to achieve success. It is estimated that 90 percent of people gave up just about the time they were ready to succeed. If they had only kept on going . . .

To illustrate this point, I give students the success quiz that follows. As I read the statements about each of these real people, students decide whether or not the person was a success or failure in his or her field. Try the quiz yourself before using it with your students. Are you able to figure out the person being described? I hope you will add others, famous or not, to the list.

Who Is a Success? Who Is a Failure?

Artist: All he wanted to do was to sketch cartoons. He applied with a Kansas City newspaper. The editor said, "It's easy to see from these sketches that you have no talent." No studio would give him a job. He ended up doing publicity work for a church in an old, dilapidated garage.

Writer: Living in a car, trying to make ends meet, this writer was persistent in contacting publishers to get his first book published. The book was rejected by twenty-three publishers.

Athlete: As a baseball player, he once held the record for striking out more than any player in the history of baseball—1,330 times.

Politician: This person was defeated seven times in running for election to political office.

Athlete: This person missed his target 9,000 times and lost 300 games.

So, what were your answers? Whether you answered success or failure, you're right! Each of these people was both a failure and success.

Here's a sampling of the conversation I have with students after they have participated in this activity:

> Let me ask you this: would you have kept on playing baseball if you struck out 1,330 times? Babe Ruth did and wound up with 714 home runs. Would you have kept on in politics if you were defeated seven times? I am so glad that Abraham Lincoln didn't give up. Would you have given up on the third time, the fourth, or the sixth? Abe hung in there and succeeded in becoming the sixteenth president, one of the most respected presidents of the United States.
>
> And what about the cartoonist no one would hire? The one who was told he had no talent? The old garage he worked in was in such bad shape

that it had mice. One day, he sketched one of those mice. Any guesses as to the name of that mouse? The mouse one day became famous as Mickey Mouse. The artist, of course, was Walt Disney.

Who was the writer whose children's book was rejected by twenty-three publishers? Take a wild guess. Yes, it was Dr. Seuss. By the way, the twenty-fourth publisher sold six million copies of And to Think That I Saw It on Mulberry Street *[1937].*

And NBA great Michael Jordan [n.d.] once said, "I have missed more than 9,000 shots in my career. I have lost almost 300 games. On 26 occasions, I have been entrusted with the game winning shot . . . and I missed. I have failed over and over and over again in my life. And that is precisely why I succeed."

Successful people never give in. They just keep on going and going, and here is why: failure is a part of success. Successful people expect to fail.

You cannot choose when success is going to be, so you have to keep on going, keep on giving, and keep on practicing. By doing so you will be ready for that moment when success comes.

These are great points to ponder, and they lead perfectly into our next discussion about failure—our best teacher!

Lesson Four: Failure Is Our Best Teacher

Failure is an important aspect of all that we do in education. It is a big part of the process that helps stimulate and cement learning. Yet our educational system is and continues to be fixated on *right answers*. Not embracing failure is enormously deceiving to students and builds resistance and fear into their perceptions of failure. Ultimately, fear of failure paralyzes students from asking questions and attempting to answer them. Students learn the lesson of *being right*. Because they fear failure and see it as the enemy of their potential success, they are reluctant to take risks. Risk taking is a necessary element of successful learning.

This lesson explores failure in a new light. My goal in this lesson is for students to expect failure, to see it as an opportunity to learn, and to discuss productive ways to handle failure through perseverance. I want students to practice developing success from failures.

After giving each student a piece of paper and some colored pencils or markers, I let them know I will be revealing a word that is an important part of being able to persevere. The word is so important that I want to do more than just discuss its meaning. I want to capture their thoughts and feelings about the word on paper. I reveal the word *failure* in large, black, bold letters on the board.

I use these prompts to help them explore their association with failure:

- What experience do you think of most often when you hear the word *failure*?

- What do you remember about failing at something?
- What words come to mind when you hear the word *failure*?
- What color is failure?
- What feelings do you have about failure? Which of those feelings is the strongest?

Before sharing in a large group, students meet in small groups to discuss their word sketches. I ask one student to report general feelings and observations back to the whole class. I do this so that none of the students have to share a negative experience.

As you can imagine, students detest and fear failure. In some manner, so do adults. Isn't that so? That's where our *running stories* come in.

Here's an example that I share with the students.

> For the last week, I have recorded things both in school and out that have not gone as planned. I failed at achieving my goal.
>
> - I wanted to exercise at least four times.
> - I wanted to have my lesson plans done.
> - I did not spend as much time with my family as I should have.
> - I tried a new recipe and my family hated it.
>
> Here is the good news: I am now able to have a much better week because I have learned from my mistakes. I'm in a position to make wiser choices about my behavior and time. It's okay to feel disappointed, but my excitement for the week ahead of me overrides that!
>
> As you persist toward your goals this week, you will likely fail to accomplish some of them. Failure is not your enemy; perfection is. Not doing something because of fear of not achieving perfection is failure. Trying, failing, getting up . . . that is success!
>
> Here is what I would like you to do for the next week. I want you to keep a journal of the times you have experienced frustration or failure. I want you to record every instance. Even if it seems small, I want you to write it down. At the end of the week, we are going to record those examples on this failure chart, but right next to the failure, we are going to find one positive thing that resulted from our failure.

My Reflections on Perseverance

I am determined to understand . . .

I showed persistence today when I . . .

I believe persistence helps me to . . .

The hardest thing about persistence is . . .

When I get stuck on a problem, I try to solve it by . . .

One new strategy I used to solve a problem today was . . .

I have found the best way to stick with a challenge is . . .

When I persevere, I feel . . .

Visit **go.solution-tree.com/instruction** to download the handout *My Reflections on Perseverance*.

Student Habitude Reflection

Students can respond to these prompts for reflection on perseverance in their habitude notebooks.

Chapter Takeaway

As I wrote this chapter, I envisioned the faces of my students who had a tough time academically. For some, life at home was in shambles, and I know they came to school wondering if they would ever make it through school or sometimes a school day. I want students walking away with one big idea: they are stronger than they think they are. If I can help them find a goal, however small, that is worth striving for, I will have been successful. The experiences they have in my classroom are intended to enable them to clear the pebbles and, by doing that, cross the mountain.

Reflections

Students will respect you for your successes, but they will love you when you're vulnerable about your struggles through hard times. Your stories will add evidence to the message that can-do attitudes are not just encouraging words in stories. Whether you are running a race or working through a difficult problem in school, perseverance is the difference between success and failure. Here are some questions for your consideration as you reflect on how you will teach lessons on perseverance:

- Which of your experiences with perseverance would you be willing to share with your students? What do you think your students will glean from your experience?

- How will you introduce the topic?

- How will you handle personal questions that students might ask?

- How will you explain what you learned from these experiences?

Perseverance Resources for Students

Aldis, D. (1978). *Nothing is impossible: The story of Beatrix Potter*. Glouchester, MA: Smith.

Bennett, W. (1996). *The book of virtues*. New York: Simon & Schuster.

Brown, M. (1991). *D. W. flips*. New York: Little, Brown.

Buck, P. S. (1986). *The big wave*. New York: HarperCollins.

Bunting, E. (1990). *How many days to America? A Thanksgiving story*. Mooloolaba, Australia: Sandpiper.

Climo, S. (1999). *The little red ant and the great big crumb*. Mooloolaba, Australia: Sandpiper.

Coerr, E. (2004). *Sadako and the thousand paper cranes*. New York: Puffin Books.

dePaola, T. (1978). *Pancakes for breakfast*. Mooloolaba, Australia: Sandpiper.

Frank, A. (1982). *The diary of a young girl*. New York: Pocket Books.

Galdone, P. (2011). *The little red hen*. Boston: Houghton Mifflin Harcourt.

Gardiner, J. R. (1997). *Stone fox*. Boston: Houghton Mifflin.

George, J. C. (2003). *Julie of the wolves*. New York: HarperTeen.

Krauss, R. (2004). *Carrot seed*. Pine Plains, NY: Live Oak Media.

Krull, K. (2000). *Wilma unlimited: How Wilma Rudolph became the world's fastest woman*. Mooloolaba, Australia: Sandpiper.

Lester, J. (1999). *John Henry*. New York: Puffin Books.

MacLachlan, P. (2004). *Sarah plain and tall*. New York: HarperCollins.

Martin, J. B. (2009). *Snowflake Bentley*. Mooloolaba, Australia: Sandpiper.

McCully, A. E. (1997). *Mirette on the high wire*. New York: Puffin Books.

O'Dell, S. (2010). *Island of the blue dolphins*. Mooloolaba, Australia: Sandpiper.

Paulsen, G. (2007). *Hatchet*. New York: Simon & Schuster.

Piper, W. (2005). *The little engine that could*. New York: Philomel Books.

Pippen, S. (1997). *Scottie Pippen: Reach higher*. Lanham, MD: Taylor Trade.

Sachar, L. (2008). *Holes*. New York: Farrar, Straus & Giroux.

Sperry, A. (2008). *Call it courage*. New York: Simon Pulse.

Stevens, J. (1985). *The tortoise and the hare: An Aesop fable*. New York: Holiday House Books.

Szab, C. (2007). *Sky pioneer: A photobiography of Amelia Earhart*. Des Moines, IA: National Geographic.

Viorst, J. (2009). *Alexander and the terrible, horrible, no good, very bad day*. New York: Atheneum Books.

Williams, V. (1984). *A chair for my mother*. New York: Greenwillow Books.

Yolen, J. (1999). *Wizards hall*. Mooloolaba, Australia: Sandpiper.

Perseverance Resources for Teachers

Baccellieri, P. (2010). *Professional learning communities: Using data in decision making to improve student learning*. Huntington Beach, CA: Shell Education.

Blankstein, A. M., Houston, P. D., & Cole, R. W. (Eds.). (2009). *Building sustainable leadership capacity*. Thousand Oaks, CA: Corwin Press.

Covey, S. M. R. (2006). *The speed of trust: The one thing that changes everything*. New York: Free Press.

Goldsmith, M., & Reiter, M. (2007). *What got you here won't get you there: How successful people become even more successful*. New York: Hyperion.

Grant, C. A. (2009). *Teach! Change! Empower! Solutions for closing the achievement gaps*. Thousand Oaks, CA: Corwin Press.

Jones, C., & Vreeman, M. (2008). *Instructional coaches and classroom teachers: Sharing the road to success*. Huntington Beach, CA: Shell Education.

Kanold, T. D. (2011). *The five disciplines of PLC leaders*. Bloomington, IN: Solution Tree Press.

Muhammad, A. (2009). *Transforming school culture: How to overcome staff division*. Bloomington, IN: Solution Tree Press.

Sobel, D. (1996). *Longitude: The true story of a lone genius who solved the greatest scientific problem of his time*. New York: Penguin.

Zander, R. S., & Zander, B. (2000). *The art of possibility: Transforming professional and person life*. New York: Penguin.

Zmuda, A., Kuklis, R., & Kline, E. (2004). *Transforming schools: Creating a culture of continuous improvement*. Alexandria, VA: Association for Supervision and Curriculum Development.

CHAPTER 6

Courage

*All our dreams can come true, if we have
the courage to pursue them.*
— WALT DISNEY

The importance of courage as a habitude became clear to me in a most unlikely way. I took my young niece, Katherine, to a local water park famous for its monster-sized waterslide. I watched her closely as she began to make the climb to the top of what seemed like Mount Everest. Each footstep became slower, softer, and smaller as she crept closer to the edge.

As she peered over and looked down, she paused briefly, her fear apparent. Yet with one deep breath, she looked at me and took the plunge!

As I met her at the bottom of the ride (yep, I turned around and walked back down), her first words to me were, "Auntie A, you missed it. That was the best ride of my whole life. You should have done it with me!"

Although these words did not give me the courage to take the plunge myself, they did get me thinking about the role fear has on living and learning. How many *rides* have I missed because I was too scared to take the plunge or step out of my comfort zone? How many times have you let *woulda, coulda, shoulda* stand in the way of taking the ride of your life? Let's consider the definition of courage and how this habitude applies to these questions:

> Courage is the ability to enter the unknown by confronting challenges, taking risks, and overcoming fears.

Katherine's story teaches a valuable lesson about courage. Students are willing and able to take the ride and risk outside of school but don't transfer that same willingness to plunge within the confines of classroom work. When confronted with risk and challenge, they hesitate as they consider the consequences of looking incompetent, struggling, or not understanding. Over time, optimism turns to pessimism, embarrassment, and ultimately learning defeat.

My goal in this chapter is to bring the childlike mindset we see in amusement parks into the classroom, where fearless learning is the norm rather than the exception.

The Pitch: Why Courage Matters

Without courage, you can do nothing worthwhile. Courage enables us to manifest something real out of a dream. Talent and skill need courage. It is the stiff backbone that helps lift the task of promoting, depending, and making good on our sense of purpose. Courage is the way to reach your potential.

We want our students to use their imagination and curiosity to dream, but they must be willing to go beyond those visions to turn their dreams into reality. I consider six essential steps students must be aware of if they are to have the courage to pursue their dreams:

1. They must know how to envision and dream.

2. They must be willing to work.

3. They must stay committed and be willing to take a stand on what is most important.

4. They must look for strength inside rather than outside of themselves.

5. They must be willing to get uncomfortable.

6. They must believe they can be bigger than they are.

Our students don't need to make headlines or engage in sensationalized endeavors to become students of courage. They just need to be willing to do the work necessary to reach their potential.

The Anchor: The Million-Dollar Conversation Starter

When is the last time you used the word *courage* in your classroom? It's a magnificent word. It's a *big* word. Yet it's a word that is difficult to define and teach. For many, courage means risking or giving one's life for others. These actions of heroism and bravery will always be deeply respected, as they touch every one of us to the core. But there is more to courage than unique feats of heroism. What do we know about everyday courage? What does it look like? What is intellectual courage? How do we recognize it? What devoted actions made by ordinary people in ordinary situations would be considered courageous?

The answers to these questions are what I seek to quantify in this first lesson, designed to help students define for themselves the true meaning of courage. I begin the lesson on courage by asking students to consider three questions:

1. When I say the word *courage*, what do you start thinking about?

2. What do you feel?

3. What do you see in your mind?

As students share probable stories of heroism and bravery, fictional or real, I acknowledge and validate how most of the world perceives courage and courageous behavior. I record their answers and images on a chart.

At this point in the lesson, I share with the group several definitions of courage, each revealing a significant behavior or attitude such as taking risks, being confident, or facing a fear. Any quotes on courage can be used, but here are a few to help you get started with your students.

What Some People Say About Courage

Courage is not the absence of fear, but rather the judgment that something else is more important than fear. —Ambrose Redmond

Success is not final, failure is not fatal: it is the courage to continue that counts. —Winston Churchill

Courage is never to let your actions be influenced by your fears. —Arthur Koestler

With courage you will dare to take risks, have the strength to be compassionate, and the wisdom to be humble. Courage is the foundation of integrity. —Keshavan Nair

Personal mastery teaches us to choose. Choosing is a courageous act; picking the results and actions which you will make into your destiny. —Peter Senge

Courage is not the lack of fear. It is the acting in spite of it. —Mark Twain

Courage is fear holding on a minute longer. —George S. Patton

I remind students that courage is not a single attribute or a recipe, but a cluster of strengths. From their discussion of the quotes, I have the students develop a list of courage attributes, which I record on a chart. The following list is a representation of student discussions about how courage is displayed.

We display courage when we:

- Allow failure

- Learn from bad decisions

- Listen intently to ideas and opinions that differ from ours

- Become honest with ourselves, taking responsibility for outcomes whether they are positive or not

- Remain confident in the face of opposition, internal or external

My conversation with the students continues in this way:

From our discussions, we now know that gaining courage is not something that happens in a day, a week, or even a year. It is an ongoing process throughout our lives. It is found not by looking for it but rather from consistent efforts toward courage-building behaviors.

So, as we study these behaviors and attributes over the next few weeks, your job will be to recognize when you see courage at work in yourself and others. We will be keeping a courage journal, so that both in and outside of school you have a place to record your observations. Let's start today.

Take the next few minutes, and create your first journal entry. Choose one courage attribute that you see in your own learning life. I will be keeping a journal as well and look forward to sharing my entry with you tomorrow.

I keep the habitudes notebook or journal handy at all times so students get accustomed to linking specific behaviors and actions with the habitude they are currently studying—courage, in this case. As examples become more concrete, students begin to recognize that courage becomes a way of acting and being rather than an abstract concept of thinking. It is important that you maintain a journal alongside your students and share your entries. In so doing, you model the kind of reflection and conscious attention to behaviors that you want students to be aware of.

Conversations That Last: Continuing the Dialogue

Courage cannot be mastered. It develops over time and with practice. The courage lessons that follow provide you with specific ideas and tools to build courage. These lessons do not follow a prescribed scope and sequence. They can and should be expanded and extended over days and weeks. These conversations keep the habitude alive and moving, enabling students to link courage to their work at school and to their lives.

Lesson One: Looking Fear in the Face

You gain strength, courage and confidence by every experience in which you really stop to look fear in the face. You are able to say to yourself, I have lived through this horror. I can take the next thing that comes along. You must do the thing you think you cannot do.

—ELEANOR ROOSEVELT

Fear. The word itself scares me. Say it, *fear.* Scary, isn't it? Yet fear is something we all have to face. It is the universal equalizer. Regardless of age, occupation, gender, or status, fear has the power to make the strongest among us weak—that is, if we let it.

This lesson is not about helping students avoid fear but rather about becoming aware of how to face it head on. Whether it is fear of failure, of rejection, of humiliation, or even of fear itself, facing your fear is the quickest way to build courage.

I wonder what our students' learning lives would be if these fears could be controlled and monitored. Let's consider the conversation I have with my students.

We have something important to address in our conversations about courage, specifically, the way successful learners handle fear. Let's talk about that today, shall we? My goals at the end of our conversation are these:

- *You will have new insight into how you look at fear and its role in your learning.*

- *You will understand what is involved and expected in fearless learning.*

- *You will have tools that you can use immediately when you see fear getting in the way of pursuing your goals.*

Here's the deal. Fear is a reality for all learners. Getting As does not make you a fearless learner: it is your attitude, mindset, and behaviors that will equip you to handle your fears. Courage is defined by how you handle fear.

Being fearless requires that we know ourselves, face ourselves, and, more importantly, trust ourselves. When we are fearless, we're more likely to accept the existence of fear; we accept that things sometimes fall apart, but we move ahead anyway.

The more often we fail and recover, the more we learn how to be successful. It's when we fail and then fail to recover, that we get stuck in fear, and it becomes our master.

To be fearless learners, you must understand:

- *Fear is a natural emotion—even the most courageous among us fear something. The difference is they do not let the fear paralyze them.*

- *Get to know your fear. Accept it. Embrace it. By doing so, you can overcome it.*

- *Things will happen. It's inevitable. And you won't like some of those things, but you will deal with them when they happen.*

- *You are capable and smart individuals. Everything you need to cope is inside you.*

- *You will have friends and classmates who will support you. You cannot handle everything alone. A huge step in becoming fearless is knowing how to create a strong network of support.*

- *Messing up is not the end, it is only a step in a direction. You have the power to choose that direction, either forward or backward. The choice is yours.*

When you face your fears, you begin to realize that things aren't as scary as you once thought. You become able to tackle bigger and better tasks and projects, even in the face of uncertainty, intimidation, and even more fear!

Today, in your courage journal, I want you to write about one of your biggest fears. This will not be shared with the group unless you choose to do so.

Tomorrow's lessons will explore specific steps to help you accept and work through that fear and explore the tools that give you confidence.

Lesson Two: Using Strong and Weak Words

Before moving into this lesson, I spend some time having the students recall and comment on our previous discussions about courage and fear. If students want to share additional experiences about the topic, I encourage them to do so. Then I move on to this lesson in which we explore the impact of words on our actions and thinking. Throughout the lesson, I provide opportunities for students to share their ideas with a partner or in small groups.

Here's my conversation with the students about how words can affect the way we behave:

Words have enormous power. The words and phrases we use can move us forward or set us backward in our thinking and actions. The good news is that we have the power to select our words. It is very important that we choose words that give us courage; I call these strong words. We must also be aware of and try to avoid any words that strip us of our confidence; let's call those weak words.

Let's explore the difference with the word lucky. *Do you think the word* lucky *is a strong word or a weak word?*

When you say someone is lucky when he or she has achieved success, you are making an excuse for that person's achievement. This excuse ignores the fact that the individual has earned and deserves success. Attributing someone's success to luck does not help that person feel more confident or courageous. It makes them feel like they did not work hard or may not deserve what they have accomplished. Lucky *is a weak word.*

Let's create a list of all words that make us feel weak, worried, and unsure of ourselves. Some of these words are maybe, if only, I fear, possibly, well, scary, could have, okay, and but. We can also think about strong words, ones that fill us with courage, hope, and power. Examples of these words are yes, can, will, someday, great, working on it, definitely, and of course. Let's work together to add words to each column. We'll discuss how these words can affect the way we think about ourselves.

Feel free to have your students brainstorm, collect, or create images that evoke the essence of each habitude in action. Images can be selected from web-based sources such as the following:

- Flickr—www.flickr.com
- Clipart—www.clipart.com/en/
- Google images—www.google.com/imghp

Students can also create their own original sketches and artwork.

This lesson keeps the conversation about courage moving forward. I encourage lots of discussion to maintain the momentum needed for students to realize the importance of courage in their lives. During the discussions about weak and strong words, I remind students how such words can affect their attitudes and behaviors. I encourage them to focus on strong words that foster courage and self-reliance.

Lesson Three: Getting Comfortable With Being Uncomfortable

Be willing to be uncomfortable. Be comfortable being uncomfortable. It may get tough, but is a small price to pay for living a dream.
— PETER MCWILLIAMS

This courage lesson is a lesson in reassociation in which I use activities designed to have students move out of their comfort zones and develop ways of dealing with discomfort. When students experience discomfort, they recognize struggle as a natural and necessary part of learning. Courage is the weapon they need to fight complacency, conformity, and disengagement.

From an early age our students are taught:

- Comfortable is the equivalent of good—it's pleasurable.
- Uncomfortable is the equivalent of bad—it's stressful and makes one unhappy.

In the 21st century, safe and comfortable could be the greatest risks our learners face. Let's talk frankly about what being comfortable means in a 21st century learning context. When students get too comfortable—learning just the basics, doing just enough to get by—they are at risk for:

- Boredom
- Complacency
- Disengagement
- Disinterest
- Lack of challenge
- Lack of motivation
- Resistance to change

Such factors, if sustained, can have long-term adverse effects on students' achievement and success in school. Helping students develop the habitude of courage is an effective way to overcome these negatives that come with being too comfortable.

Here's how I work with the students on the ideas of comfort and discomfort in learning.

You know how sometimes I start the day by saying, "Let's get comfortable"? Are you comfortable? Well, today, I have a new question for you. When is the last time you have been uncomfortable? I don't mean the chair you are sitting in or the temperature of the room; I mean in your brain, in your learning. When is the last time that you felt stretched and challenged and experienced discomfort?

I am going to ask you—no, I am going to require you—to get uncomfortable—with learning, that is.

Now, I know many of you are thinking that this does not make sense. Why would Mrs. Maiers want learning for us to be uncomfortable? Doesn't she want us to succeed and be happy as learners?

I know exactly what I am asking you to do. I absolutely want you to feel successful and happy as learners. What I do not want to see happen is for you to choose easy tasks, to take the easy road, or to do the bare minimum to get by just so that you can feel comfortable.

Learning is hard. Sometimes it even hurts because things don't go smoothly. This is where courage is needed. You have to become accustomed and comfortable in the times when things are not going smoothly and when challenge is present. You have to learn to be comfortable when learning is uncomfortable.

Here's the important point: it is during the uncomfortable moments of frustration and despair that learners quit. They say: "I don't get it. I can't do this. I don't need to know this. I don't care anymore." They do not have the strength or courage to stick it out and work through the challenges. They are not comfortable with being uncomfortable—they just want to know the quick and easy solution.

Let's think about your experiences with difficult and challenging times in your learning. You can write about these in your habitudes notebook, or you can talk about them with a partner or the group. We can use these questions to organize our thinking about the experience:

- *What was the experience?*
- *How did you respond in the midst of the struggle? Did you quit? Did you stick with the task? How did you feel about your actions?*
- *What strategies did you use? Did these strategies help or hinder?*

When you see the word comfortable, *I want you to associate these words with it:*

- Boredom
- Complacency

- Overconfidence
- Stunted
- Closed minded

As learners, you put yourself at risk of falling into these learning traps when you do not expose yourself to challenge and discomfort.

When you start to feel discomfort, start telling yourself this:

- *I am learning.*
- *I am stretching myself.*
- *My brain is getting smarter.*
- *This is soooo good for me.*
- *Growth cannot happen without discomfort.*
- *My brain gets stronger every time I challenge it.*

If we do the same things every day, we are not really growing. We only learn and grow when we are challenged to expand our comfort zones. So, this week I challenge you to be uncomfortable! Do something at least once a day that may make you uncomfortable, and write about it in your habitude notebook. Let's brainstorm a quick list of learning possibilities to get you started.

- *Teach a classmate how to do something.*
- *Speak publicly—ask for a few minutes to share or teach the class.*
- *Learn a new skill or strategy.*
- *Draw something.*
- *Become a character—act out a scene in a book or movie.*

You build your courage muscle like any other in your body—the more you stretch it, the more you work it out, the stronger it becomes. Muscle and brainwork require lifelong maintenance. Just because you lifted weights once does not give you strength for life. Stretching and building your courage is a daily, lifelong workout!

Lesson Four: Knowing Everyday Heroes

> *I long to accomplish a great and noble task, but it is my chief duty to accomplish humble tasks as though they were great and noble. The world is moved along not only by mighty shoves of heroes, but also by the aggregate of the tiny pushes of each honest worker.*
>
> —HELEN KELLER

We are a society of hero worshippers. Adoration and devotion are given to those who survive forty days on a desert island or display their life in front of a camera for millions to watch. It is no wonder students confuse idols and heroes.

In this lesson, I want students to recognize what Helen Keller so eloquently spoke of—how heroism and courage come in our everyday acts, not during sensationalized bouts of fame and fortune.

Here's how I handle the lesson with my students.

We've had some amazing discussions about the habitude of courage, haven't we? In this final lesson, I want to leave you thinking about what courage is and is not. Courage is not something to do like a checklist you create in the morning. For example, today, I will do my homework, make my bed, brush my teeth, and, oh yes, do something courageous. Courage doesn't work that way. Courage is not a to do, it is a to be.

Let me explain. To get where you want to be in learning or life is determined by your behaviors, actions, and attitude. Courage is represented in the kind of person that you will have to be to get through the tough times and to pursue your goals.

I have made a list of adjectives that represent my to be list in my courage journal. It is a reminder to myself of the kind of person I want to be every day in every act, big or small. This list serves as a promise, almost a vow to become more like this person I want to be each day I wake up.

Mrs. Maiers' to be list:

- *A better listener*
- *Open-minded*
- *Convicted*
- *Unafraid*
- *Curious*
- *Confident*
- *Flexible*

I realize that every day my courage will be tested. As I learn and grow, I will use my to be list to guide my behaviors, actions, and attitude as I move forward through obstacles and challenges I face.

Who can guess what your final entry in your courage journal will be? You got it. I want you to create your to be list. Make it big, use powerful adjectives, and be specific! You chose the words that will influence the kind of courage you can have—be picky and proud!

Student Habitude Reflection

Students can respond to these prompts for reflection on courage in their habitude notebooks.

My Reflections on Courage

I believe I am a courageous learner because . . .

I showed great courage when I . . .

I know that I am taking a responsible risk with my learning today when I . . .

When I respond to a challenge, I am able to . . .

New adventures in learning help me to . . .

When I try something new, I feel . . .

I overcame a time when I was scared by . . .

These are the people I know who dare to do things differently . . .

I dared to be different today as I was learning by . . .

Visit **go.solution-tree.com/instruction** to download the handout *My Reflections on Courage*.

Chapter Takeaway

During the Great Depression, Thomas Edison delivered his last public message. In it he said,

> My message to you is: Be Courageous! I have lived a long time. I have seen history repeat itself again and again. I have seen many depressions in business. America has always come out stronger and more prosperous. Be brave as your fathers before you. Have faith! Go forward! (as cited in Gelb & Caldicott, 2007, p. 37)

Edison knew then that courage is the force that propels us forward into and onto more powerful things. Courage, like all other habitudes, is not something you can give students. It is something that must come from within. As you strive to do what is right and best, it is my hope that these conversations show students that the decisions made every day are an investment in courage. There is no other way to reach their potential.

Reflections

The heart of education is an education of the heart.

The root of the word *courage* is the Latin word *cor*, meaning "heart." The English word *core* comes from the same Latin root. At its core, teaching is about developing courage.

Unfortunately, much of our teaching is devoted not to the heart but to the mind. We develop the intellect to solve a differential equation, to analyze and evaluate literature, and to classify differences between rocks and minerals.

The lessons in this chapter serve not only to complement these intellectual objectives but to remind us of the need to educate the heart, developing in students the courage to propose new explanations, the courage to ask new questions, and the courage to share their contributions with the world.

The heart of teaching is the teaching of the heart. In order to teach, we need courage to overcome our fears. Consider and reflect on the following statements of courage.

I have the courage to:

- Teach an unfamiliar topic and risk embarrassment when I can't answer a student's question

- Learn new, complex things and relish in the journey of the unknown and yet to be discovered

- Yield trust and control to students by listening, honoring, and recognizing their unique contributions

- Engage in discussions that challenge our deepest convictions and ignite our hidden passions

Courage Resources for Students

Baynton, M. (2007). *Jane and the dragon*. Somerville, MA: Candlewick Press.

Browne, A. (2007). *Silly Billy*. New York: Walker.

Buehner, C. (2007). *Dex, the heart of a hero*. New York: HarperCollins.

Cole, B. (2005). *Princess smartypants*. New York: Putnam.

Cutler, J. (2004). *The cello of Mr. O*. New York: Puffin Books.

de Deu Prats, J. (2005). *Sebastian's roller skates*. San Diego, CA: Kane/Miller.

dePaola, T. (1979). *Oliver Button is a sissy*. Mooloolaba, Australia: Sandpiper.

Dunbar, P. (2005). *Flyaway Katie*. New York: Walker Books.

Frazee, M. (2006). *Walk on: A guide for babies of all ages*. Boston: Harcourt.

Kelle, H. (2002). *Brave Horace*. New York: Scholastic.

McKissack, P. (2000). *Color me dark: The diary of Nellie Lee Love—The great migration north, Chicago, Illinois, 1919*. New York: Scholastic.

McPhail, D. (2011). *The searcher and the old tree*. Watertown, MA: Charlesbridge.

Naylor, P. R. (1998). *The fear place*. New York: Aladdin.

Neubecker, R. (2006). *Courage of the blue boy*. New York: Tricycle Press.

Paulsen, G. (2002). *Guts*. New York: Laurel-Leaf Books.

Paulsen, G. (2007). *Hatchet*. New York: Simon & Schuster.

Rayner, C. (2006). *Augustus and his smile*. Intercourse, PA: Good Books.

Sperry, A. (2008). *Call it courage*. New York: Simon Pulse.

Spinelli, E. (1996). *Somebody loves you, Mr. Hatch*. New York: Simon & Schuster.

Tauss, M. (2005). *Superhero*. New York: Scholastic.

Wilson, D. L. (2010). *I rode a horse of milk white jade*. Naperville, IL: Sourcebooks Jabberwocky.

Wolff, F., & Savitz, H. (2005). *Is a worry worrying you?* Terre Haute, IN: Tanglewood Press.

Courage Resources for Teachers

Brokaw, T. (1998). *The greatest generation*. New York: Random House.

Chang, J. (2003). *Wild swans: Three daughters of China*. New York: Touchstone.

Galloway, S. (2008). *The cellist of Sarajevo*. New York: Riverhead.

Hill, L. (2007). *Someone knows my name*. New York: Norton.

Hillenbrand, L. (2010). *Unbroken: A World War II story of survival, resilience, and redemption*. New York: Random House.

Nafisi, A. (2008). *Reading Lolita in Tehran: A memoir in books*. New York: Random House.

Patterson, K., Grenny, J., Maxfield, D., McMillan, R., & Switzler. A. (2008). *Influencer: The power to change anything*. New York: McGraw-Hill.

Pink, D. (2009). *Drive: The surprising truth about what motivates us*. New York: Riverhead.

Sullivan, P. (2010). *Clutch: Why some people excel under pressure and others don't*. New York: Penguin.

Wagner, J. (1994). *Edith Ann: My life so far. As told to Jane Wagner*. New York: Hyperion.

CHAPTER 7
Passion

It is our passions that will focus us and energize us in a world where those without passion will be increasingly marginalized and overwhelmed.

— JOHN HAGEL

The 21st century has been labeled many things: the Information Age, the Digital Age, and the Age of Globalization. Few would argue the world our students enter is far different from the industrialized world you and I grew up to know. In this chapter, I want to make the case that we have also entered the *age of meaning*. The need to matter—to be meaningful—is as basic and primal as our need for food, lodging, and safety. Our students need to have opportunities in school to find out what it means to care deeply about something, to have something in their lives that really matters to them. In this context, let's review the definition of the habitude of passion:

> Passion is the ability to intentionally pursue actions that are personally and socially meaningful.

Pursuing a passion-driven life—making a meaningful contribution to society and exercising our creative powers by means of sharing our individual uniqueness and brilliance with the world—is not optional: it is essential to survive and thrive in the age of meaning. Think about your own life and the passions that have influenced your choices and your decisions. Did you become a teacher because you have a passion for learning? If so, how has that element of your character influenced the way you interact with your students and colleagues? Undoubtedly, your students exhibit an array of passions that may or may not be cultivated at school or at home. A question for consideration is: should all passions be cultivated? I hope the lessons in this chapter will foster your students' understanding of the value of being intensely interested and inquisitive along with the desire to be passionate about learning.

The Pitch: Why Passion Matters

Our students will pursue their passion in an ever-changing world. The stage is interactive, and the audience is global and interactive. Competition for attention, jobs, and breakthroughs will be immense. Students who believe in themselves and their mission, persevere, and then transfer that belief and persistence in multiple modes of messaging and communication will embrace the challenges and thrive. Those who are timid, who are unwilling to share and work collaboratively, or who choose to live without passion will be left behind.

The conversations, lessons, and strategies in this chapter focus on passion to:

- Ignite curiosity
- Provide energy
- Promote collaboration
- Secure loyalty
- Act courageously
- Solve complex problems
- Remind us we are living lives that matter

As you work through these lessons with your students, you will help them become more conversant with strategies that enable them to direct their passions in ways that enhance their learning and maybe even their popularity.

The Anchor: The Million-Dollar Conversation Starter

Prior to presenting this anchor lesson, I usually spend time talking with the students about what it means to be passionate about something and how that passion is revealed. What follows is the conversation I conduct to have students elaborate on their understanding of passion.

We have quite a discussion in store for our work today. We have spent some time talking about what passion is and what it is not. I would like to take our conversation a bit deeper. Talk with your neighbor for a moment, and ponder this:

- *What is life's single most important question?*

There are many important and worthy ones—questions about family, relationships, school, work, love. But when it comes to charting your futures, one question rises above the rest. Can you guess what that question is?

- *What's your passion?*

Have you heard people talk about this before? It may sound kind of silly, even funny to some people, but it happens to be the most important question for you to think about and seek answers to. How can we describe passion?

Passion—that awesome, excited, almost uncontrollable enthusiasm that we feel about the work we are doing or the talent we have—will form the foundation for all excellence, no matter who you are.

Science shows us that passion functions in our brains like fuel; with it, we have energy and can work like there is no limit to what we can do. Without it, our minds and our bodies become weak, and all we do becomes a struggle.

We are going to explore this important question together over the next few weeks. We'll also explore a few other big questions such as:

- *How do we know when we've got passion?*
- *What do I do to keep my passion fueled?*
- *How do I find other passionate people to work with and learn from?*
- *What can I use my passion to accomplish?*

The sooner we are able answer questions like these, the sooner we are able to rocket ourselves beyond our wildest imaginations. I am so excited to get started, aren't you?

Conversations That Last: Continuing the Dialogue

Like the previous habitudes, passion is not something that one perfects or masters. We all have the capacity to become passionate about some element of the world we live in. The lessons in this chapter will help you rediscover yours and cultivate your students' passions, turning them into potential and possibility.

Lesson One: Let's Talk About Passion

To begin this conversation, I start by addressing the students as *passionate learners*. Sometimes that greeting elicits various reactions, which shows me that the students are paying attention. The conversation about passion goes as follows:

As I promised, we are going to be having some very powerful conversations over the next several weeks about the importance and role of passion in our learning and lives. To prepare for our work ahead, I did some research and found some interesting things about the word passion. *Passion is a very, very popular topic. I'll demonstrate the Google search for passion and see what we discover. Are you surprised to see there are over 150 million people talking about the importance of passion?*

I've also discovered that passion means many things to many people. Here were some of the most popular things people were saying:

- *Passion is pure joy and happiness.*
- *Passion is doing work I love.*

- *Passion is like a magnet—when you see it, hear it . . . you want some of it.*
- *Passion gives you energy and power.*
- *Passion helps you overcome obstacles.*
- *Passion is using and giving your whole heart and mind to something.*

What does passion mean to you?

While you are thinking about your answer to that question, I'm going to share with you a dictionary definition of passion:

> Passion*—intense, driving, or overmastering feeling or conviction; a strong liking or desire for or devotion to some activity, object or concept; an object of desire or deep interest [Passion, 2012].*

> *Synonyms for passion:* enthusiasm, eagerness, love, zeal, spirit, fascination, obsession, fixation, addiction, preoccupation.

That is a lot to think about for one simple word, and I want to give you time to do that alone and with your classmates. We will use a Passion Gallery Walk for this activity. You will notice that I have placed several large pieces of paper around the classroom. You will find several quotes revealing what people in the world think about the word passion. Read the quotes out loud, and think about the way they describe passion and the role passion plays in their lives and learning.

I would like you to spend a few minutes comparing the ideas in the quotes to what we talked about this morning. If there are any words or images that connect with the quote you are reading, please add those to the chart paper.

When we have finished, we will have a much clearer picture of what passion means and how we are going to think and talk about this important word in the weeks ahead.

To get you started, I have gathered the following quotes on passion, some of which I have used with students. Feel free to add your own or adapt according to grade-level needs.

Quotes and Thoughts on Passion

The most powerful weapon on earth is the human soul on fire.
—Ferdinand Foch

Nothing great in the world has been accomplished without passion.
—George Wilhelm

A genuine passion is like a mountain stream; it admits of no impediment; it cannot go backward; it must go forward.—Christian Nestell Bovee

Don't ask what the world needs. Ask what makes you come alive, and go do it. Because what the world needs is people who have come alive.—Harold Whitman

Without passion man is a mere latent force and possibility, like the flint which awaits the shock of the iron before it can give forth its spark.—Amiel

One person with passion is better than forty people merely interested.—E. M. Forster

Without passion you don't have energy, without energy you have nothing.—Donald Trump

A great leader's courage to fulfill his vision comes from passion, not position.—John Maxwell

Passion is energy. Feel the power that comes from focusing on what excites you.—Oprah Winfrey

Develop a passion for learning. If you do, you will never cease to grow.—Anthony J. D'Angelo

Love life, engage in it, give it all you've got. Love it with a passion, because life truly does give back, many times over, what you put into it!—Maya Angelou

Lesson Two: Let's Detect Your Passion

When we find the thing that makes us tick, we find our true self and purpose. We are in an unshakable place where we feel sure about who we are and what we are doing. Sir Ken Robinson (2009) calls this living in our *Element*. It is the discovery and ability to use our unique form of genius and talent toward work and learning that matters. Robinson states:

> Some of the elements of our growth are inside us. They include the need to develop our unique natural aptitudes and personal passions. Finding and nurturing them is the surest way to ensure our growth and fulfillment as individuals. If we discover the Element in ourselves and encourage others to find theirs, the opportunities for growth are infinite. (2009, p. 259)

This discovery gives us a level of confidence that most people lack because they've never gone looking for it. We're unshakable in this place. It's a place of inner knowing where we feel sure about who we are and what we're doing. Robinson's views on the importance of knowing yourself and your passions are presented in the TED Talk, Bring on the Learning Revolution (posted May 2004), which you can access by visiting www.ted.com/talks/lang /en/sir_ken_robinson_bring_on_the_revolution.html or scanning this code.

As educators, we can help our students find their element by promoting a level of self-awareness and self-assurance about what their passions and talents may be. But first, it will be helpful for you to discover the element in yourself: who you really are and what you can really do. Before presenting this lesson to your students, I recommend that you complete the following exercise, A Passion Detector. Subsequently, as appropriate, you can use the questionnaire with your students. These statements can help you detect your passion:

1. I think a lot about . . .

2. When I . . . , it gives me a deep satisfaction and sense of accomplishment.

3. Every time I see . . . , I want to know more, I want to figure out how it's done, I want to do that!

4. My friends and family think I'm kind of silly; I cannot stop talking about, thinking about, dreaming about . . .

5. I would do . . . for free, even if nobody were watching.

6. When I'm doing . . . , I am the happiest and most engaged.

7. When I'm doing . . . , it's as if I'm in a private world. Time flies.

8. If I could do or be anything, it would most definitely be . . .

9. I feel the most proud, excited, accomplished when I am doing . . .

10. I wake up thinking about . . .

Visit **go.solution-tree.com/instruction** to download the handout *A Passion Detector*.

Here's the conversation I have with students about detecting their passions.

> Discovering your true passion is neither simple nor fast. Many people search their entire lives and still cannot answer the question, What am I passionate about? And even those who have found success through their passion may still have no idea how it happened.
>
> Here's why. Passion is quiet and silent. It sneaks up on us. It operates like much like a virus when we are sick—infecting us without us knowing. Asking successful people how they got passionate is like asking people how they caught the flu. They don't know because they can't know. One day they don't have it. The next day—wham!—they do.
>
> What would be useful for most of us, I think, is some kind of passion detector: a tool that we can use to know when our fires are being lit, or a thermometer that gives the early warning signs of a passion infection. I have developed a questionnaire for you to complete. The questions will enable you to detect the potential degree of passion that you have.
>
> Look back at the responses you wrote on A Passion Detector worksheet. Here are some questions to guide your reflection:

1. *How many blanks contained the same word or topic?*

2. *What patterns were evident in the words you used?*

3. *Did you find it difficult to provide a response for some blanks? Which ones? What do you think is the source of your difficulty?*

4. *What surprised you?*

5. *What did you learn about your potential passions?*

You may be wondering what passion looks like in students. The Innovative Educator (Nielsen, 2010, 2011; http://theinnovativeeducator.blogspot.com) is a blog dedicated to sharing information, ideas, and resources among educators interested in educating innovatively—educators who are seeking the *way out of the box*. The blog features examples of profiles of passion-driven students (to explore, scan this code or go to http://theinnovativeeducator.blogspot .com/2011/01/profile-of-passion-driven-student.html; Nielsen, 2011).

Lesson Three: Let's Preserve Our Passion

In this lesson, I use a letter to educators to illustrate what we as adults can do to preserve our passion. I hope this letter will inspire you to think of ways to help your students preserve their passions.

Dear Educator,

Have you thought about your passion lately? Have you considered what gives you the energy to do what's hard? What gives you the courage to stay the course? Have you considered how your passion is being conveyed and perceived by others around you? Is passion one of your habitudes?

I'm worried about you. I see how overwhelmed you are, how frustrated and tired you are as you leave school each day. I see your passion taking second seat to the mandates and requirements.

We need schools in which everyone is joined by a passionate vision of excellence and human flourishing. We need schools in which people passionately love what they are doing, love what they are teaching, and love what they are learning. We need schools in which teachers love their colleagues, students love their teachers, teachers love their students, and parents love the school. We need schools that engender passion in everyone who is involved in the education of children.

I have found the best way to revive, reclaim, and re-energize our own passion is by connecting with other passionate people. So, I am formally inviting you to join a Passion-Driven Conversation. This Passion-Driven Conversation began when I invited a diverse group of thought leaders from across the blog world and Twittersphere to examine the topic and weigh in with their perspectives and advice. Over sixty talented writers accepted the challenge. Each came to the

continued→

conversations with their own stories and insights and examined the role passion played in their work, learning, and life (to read their stories, scan this code or visit www.angelamaiers.com).

We used the following questions as a jumping off point, and each post took the conversation (and my thinking) in a new direction. We considered questions like these:

- *What is passion . . . really?*
- *How do you define passion?*
- *How could or does passion change the game?*
- *How does passion present itself in your work? Life? Organization?*
- *What does it mean for you? Our students? Your community? Clients? The world?*
- *Can passion be taught?*
- *How is passion different than engagement?*
- *What conditions are necessary for passion to exist?*
- *Is passion a necessary or a nice-to-have quality?*
- *What are the repercussions of being a passionless person or organization?*
- *Can we quantify passion? If so, how?*
- *What is misunderstood about passion?*
- *What can we do to change this? How can we move the conversation forward?*

You'll find answers to these and other questions in a dialogue with educators discussing the impact of passion in education at http://bit.ly/zRsRVM online.

As Ken Robinson (2009) states, "Finding the Element in yourself is essential to discovering what you can really do and who you really are" (p. 251). I hope that someday we will meet in the blog world or Twittersphere and share our passions about teaching and learning.

Sincerely,

Angela Maiers

Student Habitude Reflection

Students can respond to these prompts for reflection on passion in their habitudes notebooks.

My Reflections on Passion

I love to learn about . . .

I am most passionate about . . .

These are the ideas that amaze me . . .

I look forward to learning most about . . .

I lose track of time when I am learning about . . .

I never get tired of learning about . . .

When I find myself not interested in topics, I try to . . .

How does my passion influence what I am learning about . . .

Visit **go.solution-tree.com/instruction** to download the handout *My Reflections on Passion*.

Chapter Takeaway

The 21st century poses incredible challenges and extraordinary opportunities for our students. It will require many things of us. One of them is that we become passionate people who are not afraid to ask the tough questions in our search for the best answers. As you consider time, curriculum, standards, mandates, assessments, funding, and other factors that affect you and your students, think back to the messages about passion in the previous parts of this chapter. The key point to remember is "when passion drives instruction no child is left behind" (Nielsen, 2010).

Reflections

The older I get the more I realize that the only thing a teacher has to go on is the rare spark in a child's eyes.

—LOUIS AUCHINCLOSS

In my view, the only way our students will learn as if they were to live forever is for us to provide the environment in which they can learn about themselves as well as the world they inhabit. School should do more than prepare students to be good *at school*; it should prepare them for life. Here are some questions I have used to reflect on what works and what doesn't work in school:

- Are we helping students discover and work on things they are truly good at?

- Do students go home at the end of the day emotionally charged or emotionally drained?

- Will students remember the projects we're working on today five years from now?

- Are we proud of the work we do? Are our students proud of the work they do?

- Does the *cause* for which we fight go beyond making the grade or increasing a test score?

- Does the cause create meaning in our students' lives?

If we can answer *yes* to these questions, you can be assured that your current curriculum, schedule, and classroom environment cultivate the kind of passion that will enable students to live more fulfilling lives, lead courageously, and engage in work worth bragging about!

Passion Resources for Students

Deepak, C., & Tracy, K. (2010). *On my way to a happy life*. New York: Hay House.

Hay, Louise. (2008). *I think, I am! Teaching kids the power of affirmations*. New York: Hay House.

Kranz, Linda. (2006). *Only one you*. New York: Cooper Square.

McCloud, Carol. (2007). *Have you filled a bucket today?* New York: Nelson.

McCloud, Carol. (2011). *My bucketfilling journal: 30 days to a happier life*. New York: Ferne Press.

Muth, J. J. (2002). *The three questions*. New York: Scholastic.

Stover, JoAnn. (1990). *If everybody did*. New York: JourneyForth.

Tillman, N. (2006). *On the night you were born*. New York: Feiwel & Friends

Tillman, N. (2011). *The crown on your head*. New York: Feiwel & Friends.

Passion Resources for Teachers

Bartlett, A. H. (2009). *The man who loved books too much: The true story of a thief, a detective, and a world of literary obsessions*. New York: Riverhead.

Bennett, A. (2007). *The uncommon reader*. New York: Farrar, Straus & Giroux.

Hargreaves, A. (2003). *Teaching in the knowledge society: Education in the age of insecurity*. New York: Teachers College Press.

Hess, F. M. (2010). *Education unbound: The promise and practice of Greenfield schooling*. Alexandria, VA: Association for Supervision and Curriculum Development.

Kohl, J. (2008). *A rare breed of love: The true story of Baby and the mission she inspired to help dogs everywhere*. New York: Simon & Schuster.

Maiers, A., & Sandvold, A. (2010). *The passion-driven classroom: A framework for teaching and learning*. Larchmont, NY: Eye on Education.

Manguel, A. (1998). *Into the looking-glass wood*. Toronto, ON: Knopf.

Prose, F. (2006). *Reading like a writer: A guide for people who love books and for those who want to write them*. New York: HarperCollins.

Robinson, K. (2009). *The element: How finding your passion changes everything*. New York: Penguin/Viking.

Rybczynski, W. (1991). *Waiting for the weekend*. New York: Viking.

Stigler, J. W., & Hiebert, J. (1999). *The teaching gap: Best ideas from the world's teachers for improving education in the classroom*. New York: Free Press.

Thomas, D., & Brown, J. S. (2011). *A new culture of learning: Cultivating the imagination in a world of constant change*. Charleston, SC: CreateSpace.

Wolf, M. (2007). *Proust and the squid: The story and science of the reading brain*. New York: Harper.

CHAPTER 8

Adaptability

*It is not the strongest of the species
that survives, nor the most intelligent
that survives. It is the one most
adaptable to change.*
— CHARLES DARWIN

Imagine a world that never changes. What would your life be like without the changes you have experienced over the last twenty years, twenty days, or twenty minutes? We have a love-hate relationship with change. On one hand, we greet innovation and new development with open hearts and hands. But when it comes to being the one having to do the change, change becomes an enemy. Our students are no different. With steep learning curves thrust upon them, they cling to what is most comfortable. But what does it mean to be adaptable? Let's review the definition of the habitude of adaptability:

> Adaptability is the ability to cope with change, to recognize its positive and negative aspects, and to manage one's actions to address the nature and scope of change.

Changes in technology that we witness today offer a context in which our ability to adapt may be routinely tested. How often have you heard the comment that kids are more adept with the digital world than adults? The world that today's students inhabit is significantly different from that of their parents and teachers. Youth are often described as *digital natives*, while the term *digital immigrants* is often applied to older people (Prensky, 2006; Small & Vorgan, 2008). Of course, such labels can't be universally applied; however, this distinction helps us appreciate the potential for lack of understanding in how to connect with our students. Jukes, McCain, and Crockett (2010) explain:

> What some of us don't understand is that the reason the digital generation has different skills and literacies is that there has been a profound shift in the kinds

of skills used and needed to operate in the digital world. The reason their skill development is different is because their focus is different. They are developing skills in areas other than we did and we often don't acknowledge or see the value these skills have. Instead, we complain about the skills they don't have. Because digital isn't our native language and because we're immigrants to their world, many of us believe children who act differently need to be fixed. . . . They don't need to be fixed; rather, we need to use and build on the new skills they bring to the classroom. (p. 16)

Technology is not the only factor that calls for us and our students to develop the habitude of adaptability. Change is evident in nearly every facet of our lives—family structures, work schedules, employment opportunities, social networking, immediacy of access to what is happening in the world, and so on. Adaptability for both teachers and students is more than just serving change: it is using change as a growth opportunity. In fact, you can control change by anticipating it. This kind of development requires robust adaptability. The world opens up for adaptable learners who approach each task and challenge in their learning and life with a beginner's mindset. These learners embrace challenge with openness and flexibility. Those who don't embrace change with adaptability usually get blindsided by it.

The Pitch: Why Adaptability Matters

As Darwin observed, the ability to adapt holds true in both biology and education. The concept of adaptability is not new as the pace and types of change we experience continue to grow rapidly. According to 21st Century Learning (2008), "In a global economy, workers need to be increasingly adaptable, versatile, and tolerant of uncertainty in order to operate effectively and efficiently in these changing and varied environments."

Simply put, in our world, there is only one constant: change. And that's why the adaptable will survive and thrive in change. Our 21st century learners must be able to:

- Respond favorably to change

- Handle complexity

- Solve problems critically and creatively

- Be willing to take risks

- Have confidence in their decisions

Persistent adaptability allows students to respond rather than react, reflect rather than remember, and evolve rather than atrophy. Seth Godin (2010) maintains that indispensability is the key to meeting the challenges in today's world, and that means changing one's behavior and skills. This concept might have even larger implications for your students in the future. Godin explains his views in the talk Linchpin Part 1, which you can access at this code or by going to www.youtube.com/watch?v=4fXjxHIQXGI (requires Flash).

The Anchor: The Million-Dollar Conversation Starter

How often do you think your students have encountered the terms *adaptation* or *adaptability* in classes other than science? When you are talking with students about characters in a novel, do you invite them to focus on ways in which the characters adapted their behaviors as the plot developed? In math class, do you encourage the students to adapt their strategies to find alternative ways to come up with the answers to problems? Do you encourage students to think about how they might have to change their behaviors to contribute to a positive school and classroom culture? Think about your teaching practices. How have these changed over the years? What led to those changes? How did you adapt to changes that were mandated: for example, a new curriculum, installation of a white board in your classroom, or participation in a professional learning community? There is no shortage of questions we can use to focus attention of the importance of adaptability in our lives and those of our students. In the lessons that follow, I demonstrate how I help students develop a sense of the significance of this habitude. In some cases, you may prefer to share your personal stories of how you have applied the habitude of adaptability.

Here's the conversation I like to have about adaptability with students.

Today begins our study of the habitude of adaptability. Take a minute and talk with one another about adaptability. Have you heard the word adapt *before? Why do you think being able to adapt is important to successful learning and living?*

Students shared the following ideas about adaptability:

- *It is something animals do in their environments, like chameleons—they adapt to their surroundings, right?*

- *Adaptability is part of how animals survive and live.*

- *Dinosaurs are extinct because they couldn't adapt to the land or weather.*

- *People can adapt too, like during weather. They can go from hot climates to cold.*

- *When you adapt it means you change to better fit your environment or circumstance.*

You guys are right on! Adaptability is about change and how we view the changes we want or need to make. Those changes can be something from the outside or something we want personally to improve from the inside. The habitude of adaptability has two parts:

- *First, you must be flexible and willing to adapt to the change. Having a positive attitude about the change is critical.*

- *Second, you must have the ability and the resources to handle or make the change.*

Here's why working through this habitude together is so important. Adapting to any change is difficult, even if the change is a good one. Adapting means that in some way you have to do or be something different. The problem is we like to be comfortable. We like to do things in the same way we have always done them. In our routines, we become comfortable and safe. Trying new things or doing something in a different way is hard work because you have to keep challenging yourself. If we continue to stay clear of change and hang onto what is easy and comfortable, we will never get better or stronger, or grow. And besides, change is going to happen whether we're comfortable or not.

I want to share with you a story of my adaptability.

For almost six months when I began running as part of my exercise program, I ran the same route, at the same pace, sometimes even at the same time. I got so comfortable running the same route that it wasn't even hard for me anymore. The problem was, I was not getting stronger and better as a runner. The only way that I could get better was to adapt. So, here's what I did: I added challenge to my normal running routine. Some days, I would do hills, sometimes I would run faster, sometimes longer. Even though it was hard, the adaptations I used helped me become a better runner.

Champion learners are just like that. They never let themselves get too comfortable with what they know and do. They challenge themselves by continuously adapting. When they run into a problem, they love it because it means that new, smarter learning is ahead. They are confident that any problem they encounter can be handled. Adaptive learners are lifelong learners because, for them, learning never stops. In every situation, they know there is always a way that they could do it better, smarter, faster. That is the kind of learner I know we all can be. Over the next few weeks, we are going to be learning and practicing becoming adaptive learners. The ability to adapt can be learned. As with most skills, it takes practice, practice, practice.

Here's what I would like you to do before we talk again. I want you to think of a time in your life when you have needed to make a change, like I did with my running. What helped you adapt? How was your attitude? What tools or behaviors helped you adapt successfully? Draw a picture to tell me a little about that experience. We will share those so we can learn from one another.

Conversations That Last: Continuing the Dialogue

Adaptability cannot be mastered. It develops over time and with practice. The following adaptability lessons provide you with specific ideas and tools to build adaptability. These lessons do not follow a prescribed scope and sequence. They can and should be expanded and extended over days and weeks. These conversations keep the habitude alive and moving, enabling students to link adaptability to their work at school and to their lives.

Lesson One: Picturing an Adaptive Learner

A good friend of mine is a third year medical school student. She came in excited about attending the best teaching hospital. I asked her how she was learning more there than during her previous experiences. "The answer is simple," she said.

> Before making rounds, the doctor will always go in and discuss what they can expect to see, what they want the students to notice about certain patients or situation, and then at the end of the day, there is a reflection and review on what was noticed. Now we go into the work knowing what to expect and what to look out for, so as we reflect on our work as learners, we can pinpoint the aspects of adaptability we are working towards practicing. (J. Klepic, personal communication, 2009)

We can do the same for our students. Here's what I talked about with a group of students.

> We know adaptability is important if we want to remain strong and powerful learners. In order for that to happen, in school and out, there are important things we need to be aware of. As I share a personal story about adaptability, I want you to pay close attention to the following: What challenges did I face? How did I handle those challenges? What behaviors and attitudes did you notice? After the story, we'll make a list and call it "Portrait of an Adaptive Learner."

> Here's what happened.

> My sister recently visited me. I knew she was coming, so I had prepared a special dinner for her and her family. I had carefully planned the meal for four extra people, made my grocery list, and had even begun preparing some of the food. Just hours before they arrived, some very good friends of mine dropped by. Even though I was excited to see them, I knew I had better make some changes to my dinner plans. Listen carefully to what I did, and see if you can pick out the tools I used to help me adapt.

> I noticed I started to feel frustrated. I wanted to see my friends, but I was very stressed that my sister was already on her way. So, I said to myself, "This is no big deal. We'll just have something different for dinner. I will save the food for tomorrow night."

> Next, I thought of a plan to make something that would feed more people but still be quick to fix. And I had all the ingredients I needed. By adding just a few items from the pantry and modifying how the meal was prepared (I went from a single meatloaf to lots of spaghetti), I had a whole new menu.

The students shared their observations about my behaviors. Here's what they used to create a Portrait of an Adaptive Learner:

- I changed my thinking with a better attitude.
- I problem solved without panic.
- I recreated something from inventory on hand.
- I looked at things differently.
- I recognized change was on its way, with or without my approval.
- I used some of my first dinner plans to help me with my new dinner.

Lesson Two: Stepping Outside the Box

Regardless of level or grade, students have grown accustomed to having a set of rules or constraints—a box—within which to think. By the time students are fifteen years old, they will have completed over 1500 exams with right and wrong answers. What do you think that does to their problem-solving capabilities? They have been taught to look for one right answer, when many may be possible.

Students develop a narrow-minded approach with a push for one simple solution. We complain when rigidity sets in and complain that kids do not think outside of the box. So what is the box? And what does thinking outside of it really mean? This lesson seeks to explore that with students.

One of the first lessons I teach my university students works great for introducing—both literally and figuratively—what out-of-the-box thinking is all about. This exercise is a classic, and the solution is said to have spawned the phrase *thinking outside the box*. Ready?

In front of students, I draw nine dots (see fig. 8.1).

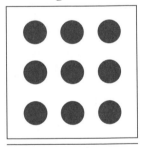

Figure 8.1: Nine dots.

Then, I ask the students to join the nine dots together by using four lines only, and to do so without taking their pen off the paper. So, how did you do? I have found that the students enjoy this exercise, and it is a great way to get the discussion brewing. One of the possible solutions is shown in figure 8.2.

Lesson Three: Turning "Yeah, Buts" Into "Yes, Hows"

We have all been there. We come up with a new idea or a creative solution, and instead of our adaptability being celebrated, we hear these two little words: "Yeah, but . . ." Or in other words, *"Are you crazy?? That will never work."* New ideas are fragile. The more creative, wild, or off the wall, the more fragile they become.

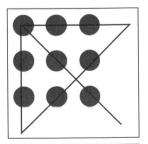

Figure 8.2: Thinking outside the box.

Fragile ideas need to be nourished. This lesson intends to keep those new and creative ideas moving forward.

The discussion helps students realize that it is far easier to kill an idea than to encourage it and turn it into a useful solution. I want them to be aware of how their language and response to new ideas can destroy discovery and breakthroughs. I tell students that ideas are like gentle flowers. In order to bloom, the flower needs tender loving care. Even a slight wrong move could stifle the flower's ability to bloom. I make the connection that new ideas are like those flowers. In the beginning stages of growth, one wrong move and we kill it.

We must be very careful with our new ideas; one wrong word has the potential to kill the best thinking we are capable of. Even if the idea seems far fetched, we will never kill the thought. Putting the words that could potentially damage or stifle a new idea on public display makes students aware of what to and what not to say. Here are some examples of our work.

To Kill an Idea, Say . . .

- Good idea, but . . .
- That sounds like too much work.
- You could never do that.
- They will never let us.
- That's not my job.
- We've never tried it that way before.
- We could never do that here.
- We tried that already.

To Nurture an Idea, Say:

- Wow, that could be very cool.
- Yes, and . . .
- That's a good idea/point/comment.
- Great, let's try it.
- How can we make time to see if it will work?
- What resources would we need to do it?
- How can we make it work?
- Let's try it out.

continued→

- What can I do to help this happen?
- I like it.
- That sounds interesting, tell me more.

From these examples, I hope you will see there are many ways in which your students can learn to be constructive in their responses to new ideas. I like to remind them of two things:

1. There are ways to encourage an idea without necessarily agreeing on action.

2. Be on a constant watch for putting down an idea too early without understanding the positive reasons for why it was suggested.

Lesson Four: Learning Lifelong Adaptability

In this lesson, students will learn a new meaning for the word *scamper*. Students assume that all problems are negative. The goal of this lesson is help them view a problem as an opportunity and use their brains in a new or different way. Successful problem solving is adaptability in action. You may have presented your students with a variety of problem-solving strategies, but sometimes a whole new approach is needed, one that students have not tried before. Sometimes, we have to stand back and try looking at the problem from different angles or perspectives. I introduce students to SCAMPER, an acronym for a collection of words that help you to think differently about a problem (Eberle, 1997; Creating Minds, 2010; http://creatingminds.org/tools/scamper.htm). The changes SCAMPER stands for are:

- **S**ubstitute—components, materials, people
- **C**ombine—mix, combine with other assemblies or services, integrate
- **A**dapt—alter, change function, use part of another element
- **M**odify—increase or reduce in scale, change shape, modify attributes (such as color)
- **P**ut to another use—reuse, other uses if modified
- **E**liminate—remove elements, simplify, reduce to core functionality
- **R**earrange—turn inside out or upside down

SCAMPER serves as a framework for adaptability in actions. That helps you think of changes you can make to an existing product to create a new one. You can use these changes either as direct suggestions or as starting points for adaptive thinking.

The SCAMPER technique consists of a set of questions that, when answered, inspire newer ideas. The procedure assumes that the answers we seek lie within the problem or task itself, and by probing a little deeper, we can find them.

To help students think about an idea, topic, or problem in a new light, ask them to consider the SCAMPER checklist of questions to see what new ideas and thoughts emerge. You'll find ideas start popping up almost immediately as you ask these questions:

- Can you substitute something?
- Can you combine your subject with something else?
- Can you adapt something to your subject?
- Can you magnify or add to it?
- Can you modify or change it in some fashion?
- Can you put it to some other use?
- Can you eliminate something from it?
- Can you rearrange it?
- What happens when you reverse it?

Visit **go.solution-tree.com/instruction** to download the handout *SCAMPER Checklist of Questions*.

Student Habitude Reflection

Students can respond to these prompts for reflection on adaptability in their habitude notebooks.

My Reflections on Adaptability

I consider myself very adaptable because . . .

I know this because . . .

A time when I was flexible and able to adapt my thinking was . . .

I consider myself a good problem solver because . . .

I looked at new ways of learning today when I . . .

Developing new problem-solving skills has helped me to . . .

I was adaptable in my thinking today when I . . .

In class today, I tried these different ways of thinking about an idea or a problem . . .

continued →

One thing that helps me think flexibly and stay adaptable is . . .

The hardest thing about modifying my thinking . . .

I have found the benefits of thinking flexibly to be . . .

Visit **go.solution-tree.com/instruction** to download the handout *My Reflections on Adaptability*.

Chapter Takeaway

Robert Sternberg (1988), a leading authority on intelligence, interviewed hundreds of people and asked them what they considered to be the central characteristics of intelligence. As you can probably guess, these are the very things we have talked about with this habitude:

- Problem solving

- Ability to change

- Creative and critical thinking

- Being comfortable to risk

- Able to handle complexity

In summarizing these characteristics, Sternberg (1988) wrote, "Intelligence is goal-directed adaptive behavior" (p. 63). I have used Sternberg's material to extend students' thinking about adaptability.

Adaptability

Being able to stretch your mind farther than you thought you could —Age 11

Being adaptable makes you more intelligent because you can handle any problem that comes your way —Age 11

How you can think of new ways of doing things —Age 7

Important so you can talk what you know and apply it to something else you are learning —Age 9

Shows you can think for yourself —Age 6

It proves how smart your brain can be if you listen to it —Age 9

How do your students define this 21st century habitude?

Reflections

Nostalgia is like a grammar lesson: You find the present tense and the past perfect.
— ROBERT ORBEN

The illiterate of the twenty-first century will not be those who cannot read and write, but those who cannot learn, unlearn, and relearn.
— ALVIN TOFFLER

It is no accident that I included the habitude of adaptability last in the list. It is the central and often most hidden factor to becoming independent and interdependent, relying both on self and others. This habitude gives students not only an educational edge but also an edge for living. This is what separates good from great, ordinary from extraordinary. By making sure this habitude is the foundation of future learning, we instill the wherewithal for our future adults to thrive and survive.

Adaptability is not just a nice-to-have competency. It is a competitive advantage for both you and your students. As you have seen, our literature and world are filled with stories of the individuals who stood up to tradition, who saw the change coming in time, who did something different, and who were able to achieve greatness because they were willing to embrace the change and adapt accordingly.

Those who are nimble, adaptable, and capable of improvising draw from each and every one of the previous habitudes, creating a broad toolbox of resources, tactics and approaches needed to thrive amid any changing circumstance.

Think about difficult change situations you have faced, and reflect on those that served you most effectively during the before, during, and after the process. Table 8.1 describes some characteristics associated with habitude of adaptability. How would you rate your adaptability on each characteristic: Very (V)? Somewhat (S)? Not at all (N)? You may want to adapt this worksheet for use with your students.

Table 8.1: My Adaptability Rating

Characteristic	Description	My Personal Ranking
Optimistic	I believe that the change will have positive outcomes. I explain issues to myself in a way that gives hope.	V S N

continued→

Characteristic	Description	My Personal Ranking
Self-assured	I believe in my own capabilities. I am in control of change rather than letting the change control me.	V S N
Focused	I am able to prioritize. I pursue goals even in the face of difficulties.	V S N
Open to ideas	I generate alternative ideas and solutions. I am prepared to use these ideas in practice.	V S N
Seeks support	I actively seek support of others in times of change. I see value in seeking the views of others.	V S N
Structured	I am able to make a plan for change for myself. I am prepared to adjust the plan.	V S N
Proactive	I am prepared to step out into the unknown. I take the necessary action to make the plan happen.	V S N

Visit **go.solution-tree.com/instruction** to download the handout *My Adaptability Rating*.

Take some time to reread and reflect on Orben's and Toffler's quotations at the beginning of this section. What was your initial reaction to the quotes? Did you think about how those words applied to you, to your students, or to your colleagues? To what extent, in your own life and in your teaching, do you think you have dealt effectively with change? What is the most important message about adaptability that you have taken away from this chapter?

Adaptability Resources for Students

Avi. (1997). *Beyond the western sea*. New York: HarperCollins.

Bauer, A. (2005). *Rules of the road*. New York: Speak.

Briggs, M. (2009). *Snowflake Bentley*. Mooloolaba, Australia: Sandpiper.

dePaola, T. (1996). *The legend of the Indian paintbrush*. New York: Puffin Books.

DiSalvo, D. (1994). *City green*. New York: HarperCollins.

Dr. Seuss. (1990). *Oh, the places you'll go*. New York: Random House.

Ephron, D. (1993). *The girl who changed the world*. New York: Houghton Mifflin.

Fleischman, P. (2002). *Weslandia*. Somerville, MA: Candlewick Press.

Gallo, D. (1999). *No easy answers: Short stories about teenagers making tough choices*. New York: Laurel-Leaf Books.

Haley, G. E. (1988). *A story, a story*. New York: Aladdin.

Hall, D. (2004). *Ox-cart man*. Pine Plains, NY: Live Oak Media.

Hamilton, V. (2000). *The girl who spun gold*. New York: Blue Sky Press.

Hopkinson, D. (1995). *Sweet Clara and the freedom quilt*. Decorah, IA: Dragonfly Books.

Jones, L. (2007). *Five brilliant scientists: Great Black heroes*. New York: Fitzgerald Books.

Kehret, P. (1997). *The richest kids in town*. New York: Aladdin.

Kurtz, J. (1998). *Fire on the mountain*. New York: Aladdin.

Polacco, P. (2001). *Thank you Mr. Falker*. New York: Philomel Books.

Polacco, P. (2004). *Betty doll*. New York: Puffin Books.

Simms, T. (1999). *Joseph had a little overcoat*. New York: Viking.

Stanley, D. (2003). *Saving sweetness*. Pine Plains, NY: Live Oak Media.

Stewart, S. (2007). *The gardener*. New York: Square Fish.

Wolff, L. (2006). *Make lemonade*. New York: Holt.

Adaptability Resources for Teachers

Adams, J. L. (1986). *Conceptual blockbusting: A guide to better ideas*. New York: Perseus.

Bellanca, J., & Brandt, R. (Eds.). (2010). *21st century skills: Rethinking how students learn*. Bloomington, IN: Solution Tree Press.

Blankstein, A. M. (2010). *Failure is not an option: 6 principles for making student success the only option* (2nd ed.). Thousand Oaks, CA: Corwin Press.

Darling-Hammond, L., & Bransford, J. (Eds.). (2005). *Preparing teachers for a changing world: What teachers should learn and be able to do*. San Francisco: Jossey-Bass.

Davidson, C. N. (2011). *Now you see it: How the brain science of attention will transform the way we live, work, and learn*. New York: Viking.

Edwards, P., & Edwards, S. (2000). *The practical dreamer's handbook: Finding the time, money, and energy to live the life you want to live*. New York: Putnam.

Goodwin, B., Lefkowits, L., Woempner, C., & Hubbell, E. (2011). *The future of schooling: Educating America in 2020*. Bloomington, IN: Solution Tree Press.

Jacobs, H. H. (Ed.). (2010). *Curriculum 21: Essential education for a changing world*. Alexandria, VA: Association for Supervision and Curriculum Development.

Johnson, S. (1998). *Who moved my cheese: An amazing way to deal with change in your work and in your life*. New York: Putnam.

Jukes, I., McCain, T., & Crockett, L. (2010). *Understanding the digital generation: Teaching and learning in the new digital landscape*. Kelowna, BC: 21st Century Fluency Project.

Perkins, D. (2000). *Archimedes' bathtub: The art and logic of breakthrough thinking*. New York: Norton.

Prensky, M. (2006). *"Don't bother me Mom—I'm learning!"* St. Paul, MN: Paragon House.

Rosen, L. D. (2010. *Rewired: Understanding the iGeneration and the way they learn*. New York: Palgrave Macmillan.

Rybczynski, W. (1986). *Home: A short history of an idea*. New York: Viking Penguin.

Small, G., & Vorgan, G. (2008). *iBrain: Surviving the technological alternation of the modern mind*. New York: HarperCollins.

Wagner, T. (2010). *The global achievement gap: Why even our best schools don't teach the new survival skills our children need—and what we can do about it*. New York: Basic Books.

Wolk, R. A. (2011). *Wasting minds: Why our education system is failing and what we can do about it*. Alexandria, VA: Association for Supervision and Curriculum Development.

Zhao, Y. (2009). *Catching up or leading the way: American education in the age of globalization*. Alexandria, VA: Association for Supervision and Curriculum Development.

CHAPTER 9

Closing Thoughts

If teachers become distant from their own learning, they will most certainly become distant from the learning of their students.

— ALISA WILLS-KEELY

Thought you were done? We're not quite finished! I have one more task before you leave our conversation. For far too long, standards, mandates, and assessments have driven what we teach, the discussions and debates we have, and the decisions we make as educators. We even define ourselves through the content we teach: "Hello, my name is Angela, and I teach literacy." We need to think differently about our practice. I invite you now and every day to think about *who* you teach and more importantly, *how* your teaching will influence *who* they are.

The Learners We Have, the Learners We Need

The students' habitude notebooks can provide you with insights into their understanding and use of the habitudes. In addition to reviewing the students' reflections on individual habitudes, you may find it useful to have them respond to a general habitudes reflection. Examples of prompts for this reflection follows.

General Habitude Reflections

Who do you know who is a lifelong learner?

What can I do to ensure that I remain a learner throughout my lifetime?

Remaining open to continuous learning is important because . . .

The habitude most significant to my success in learning is . . .

The habitude I struggle most with is . . .

I try to help myself with that habitude by . . .

Visit **go.solution-tree.com/instruction** to download the handout *General Habitude Reflections*.

Think back to your observations of your students as they participated in the habitudes lessons and other instructional activities. From your review of the material students have recorded in their habitudes notebooks, you will have gained additional insights into their views of themselves as learners. Tell me about *who* you teach. Don't make this list quickly just because you are almost done with the book. Take time to really describe and define your learners. Tell me specifically what you know about those who sit before you every day. What are they like? What do you notice about them? How would you describe them? How do they engage both inside and outside your classroom?

Examples of how other teachers have answered these questions follow. The responses are categorized by high school, middle school, and elementary school learners. What do you notice as you read through the responses? Is a pattern evident? Is this how you would describe your students?

High school and middle school learners were described as . . .

- Apathetic
- Disengaged
- Frustrated
- Unwilling to risk
- Disinterested
- Bored
- Inefficient
- Unmotivated
- Inflexible
- Shut down
- Faking it

Elementary learners (five- to twelve-year-olds) were described as . . .

- Excited
- Energetic
- Inquisitive
- Eager
- Confident
- Avid
- Passionate
- Motivated
- Flexible

- Willing to risk
- Content with ambiguity
- Problem solving
- Strategic
- Curious

Take a few moments to compare your description of your students with the preceding examples. Do you have anything in common with the educators who provided those examples? What do you think accounts for the contrasting descriptions of high school, middle school, and elementary school learners?

My goal in writing this book was to enable you to become attuned to the positive outcomes for students who learn about and embrace the habitudes: imagination, curiosity, self-awareness, perseverance, courage, passion, and adaptability. Think back to the descriptions you wrote of your students. Is a pattern evident in your descriptions? Do these descriptions provide evidence of the habitudes? Which learners do you wish your teaching produced?

Teachers typically strive for excellence in their practice and in their students' performance. Jim Collins (2001), in his book *Good to Great*, urged companies striving to become great to "engage in dialogue, not coercion; conduct autopsies without blame; and build red-flag mechanisms that turn information into information that cannot be ignored" (p. 180). These words have application to what we do in school. What can we do to take our schools and our students from good to great? Where do you find the opportunities for constructive dialogue, replacing blame with critical analysis, and drawing on data that inform decisions? If your future hopes for your learners clash with your current realities, know two things:

1. Learners come to us ready to be equipped with the habitudes we most desire.

2. You now know how to get your learners there!

If you are reading this book, you absolutely have the skills and passion (and dare I say *habitudes*) required to prepare learners for the challenges of the 21st century. Finishing this book will not be enough to change your students' lives. The habitudes are a lifestyle decision, not a curriculum. I have offered you and your students dozens of places to start, but it will be up to you to take the first steps and many steps afterward. I know that you can *sooooo* do this!

The answer to how to equip your students for future success is right in your hands and in your heart. I am amazed at how smart we can be together. Please share your habitude stories with one another. Use my lessons as jumping off points. Reframe, refine, and most importantly, share the conversations. The knowledge we need for educational reform and change will not come in the form of scary statistics or scientific research or even more habitudes lessons. It will come from these conversations.

So, I ask, even implore you to be the impetus for that change. Embody and live the habitudes you wish your students to acquire and know. Take your own life from good to great by:

1. Remaining curious

2. Using your imagination to seek new solutions

3. Persevering through the many challenges you face

4. Staying self-aware—notice what you model, monitor what you say, and seek continuous improvement in your practice

5. Embracing change by knowing you have the capacity to adapt—go forth with courage

6. Believing in your power to influence

7. Honoring your gifts and passion

8. Sharing this list with a colleague or close friend to get an outside perspective and then committing to these items as *your* habitudes

APPENDIX A
The Habitudes Notebook

The purpose of the habitudes notebook is to teach learners to take responsibility for their individual thinking and learning during the habitude study. The notebook provides students with a tool for reflection and inquiry and serves as a window into their minds as they process and apply the habitudes throughout their day. Students can record information about the lessons and class discussions in an interactive and engaging way. They can:

1. Transform important ideas and concepts into their own words

2. Record and prioritize the main points from each lesson

3. Set and organize personal goals around the habitudes

4. Make connections to success in other individuals and events

5. Creatively and strategically apply the habitudes principles throughout their own study

For teachers, the notebooks become portfolios that demonstrate students' individualized learning through content that:

- Is personal

- Is creative

- Provides evidence of growth and progress over time

- Reveals awareness of and implementation of the habitudes

- Serves as a chronological record of learning

- Can be used for review

Notebook Preparation

Have students bring a large-bound notebook or a heavy-duty three-pronged folder to class. Save five to ten pages at the front of the notebook to house information about it and a cumulative table of contents. Have them number the pages immediately so they start in an organized fashion.

Find a central location in the classroom to store the notebooks, or instruct students to bring their habitudes notebooks to class each time a lesson is taught. Encourage the students to get in the habit of reflection and reflective writing each time you meet to discuss how they are using ideas from the habitudes lessons.

If your school uses laptops for learning, or has a one-to-one laptop ratio, you may want to give students the option of keeping their reflections in an online notebook.

The notebook can be made ahead of time or tabbed with specific sections marked for each habitude as it is presented. A list of notebook components follows:

- Front cover—Have students design the cover for a more personalized and customized look and feel.

- Table of contents—List the habitudes in the order they will be studied.

- Habitudes definitions—Use the handout *Definitions and Descriptions of the Habitudes* (see table 1.1, page 19, or visit **go.solution-tree.com /instruction** to download the worksheet).

- Student habitude reflections—Use the templates provided with each habitude chapter (visit **go.solution-tree.com/instruction** to download these templates).

- Habitude self-assessment—Use the template *Habitude Definition Assessment* (see table 1.3, p. 23, or visit **go.solution-tree.com/instruction** to download the handout).

- Blank pages—Use these for notes, images, and sketches.

- Book list—Use these pages for students to list corresponding resources and materials for further reading and study.

Notebook Contents

The notebook should be the student's personalized record of habitudes learning. The contents can include a range of materials that are relevant to the individual. The notebook should hold everything when possible. Folding, cutting, and gluing are keys to its organization. As material becomes too complex, a separate folder (pocket folder) can be added to hold handouts that are multipaged. A sampling of items students can include in their notebooks follows:

- Drawings

- Images

- Quotes

- Graphic organizers

- Cartoons
- Charts
- Sketches
- Notes

Online Notebook Options

Taking the habitudes notebook online is a great way to integrate technology into your lessons. Thanks to the wonderful web, many tools are available to us. A sampling of those tools follows.

Blogs

- **Blogger**—http://blogger.com
- **Tumblr**—www.tumblr.com
- **LiveJournal**—www.livejournal.com
- **Posterous**—https://posterous.com/
- **Kidsblogs**—http://kidblog.org/home.php

Microblogs

- **Twitter**—http://twitter.com
- **Edmodo**—www.edmodo.com

Digital Notebooks and Journals

- **Evernote**—www.evernote.com
- **Penzu**—http://penzu.com/
- **My Diary**—www.my-diary.org
- **Springnote**—www.springnote.com/en

Evaluation Suggestions

How you assess notebook use is dependent on the ages and grade levels of your students. Don't feel compelled to formally grade the work; the purpose of the notebook is reflective in nature. Your attention to how the students use the notebook and your feedback about it as a learning tool can encourage students to use the tool consistently.

The following suggestions provide guidance for both formal and informal evaluation of the notebooks:

- Explain the purposes of the notebooks when you have the students create them.

- Explain at the outset the criteria on which the notebooks will be evaluated.

- Glance at the notebooks each day for the first few weeks of the semester.

- Walk around and give positive comments as students are using their notebooks.

- Use a symbol to monitor timely accomplishment of assignments.

- Build use of the notebooks into the habitudes lessons (see the Student Habitude Reflection sections in chapters 2–8).

- Schedule small-group sessions for students who need extra support in using the notebook effectively.

- Model and support note taking as appropriate for your students' ages and grade levels.

- Don't feel compelled to grade every notebook or entry—collect a few each day over a period of time.

- Require students to do a self-assessment of their notebooks.

Introducing the Notebook

An example of the narrative I use to introduce the notebook follows.

Boys and Girls,

I am excited to introduce our habitudes notebook. We will be using our notebooks during our habitudes units of study. This interactive notebook is more than a place to take notes. It is a way of collecting and processing information.

Great scholars, artists, and scientists have used notebooks like these and found them to be powerful tools to increase their knowledge, productivity, and expertise. This method of reflective thinking and learning can serve you as well.

Using your habitudes notebook has many benefits and will, in and of itself, help you develop your understanding and use of the habitudes. Using your habitudes notebook helps you:

- *Think about your thinking*

- *Apply what you are learning to your own studies*

- *Become better question-askers*

- *Tap into your creative side*

- *Remain open to continuous learning*

And I'm sure you could think of many other benefits!

This is your notebook. You are going to keep it for yourself. There is not one right way to record your thoughts and plans. It helps you process and record the important points from our conversations. More importantly, it will help you reflect on what you wish to do with that information and how you might apply the habitudes in your study and life.

This week, we will practice exploring a few tools and templates that you may want to include in your notebook. I have some examples if you would like to see how other learners have organized theirs. It is important you find something that works for you. Your notebook will be the key to your success in these lessons. At the end of the year, you will have your notes, handouts, and valuable information concerning the habitudes all in one place.

I know you will thank me later. For now, I am excited to get our notebooks organized and ready to go! It is essential before we begin our million-dollar conversations!

Habitudes Notebook Reflection Templates

The templates for the Student Habitude Reflection sections shown in chapters 2–8 are referenced in the Notebook Preparation section of this appendix (see page 129). Those templates are available for download at **go.solution-tree.com/instruction**. These additional templates are also available for download at that site.

Notebook Template 1:
The Habitude I'm Using

The Habitude I'm Using	What It Means to Me	Why It's Important	Where/When I Use It	How It Helps Me Succeed

Notebook Template 2:
How I Use the Habitudes

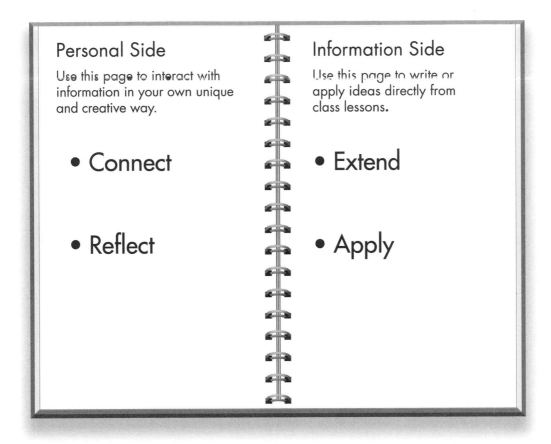

Personal Side

Use this page to interact with information in your own unique and creative way.

- Connect

- Reflect

Information Side

Use this page to write or apply ideas directly from class lessons.

- Extend

- Apply

Notebook Template 3:
My Beginning Thoughts About
the Habitudes

The habitude of _____

In my own words: _____
_____

My images: _____
_____
_____
_____

Quotes: _____
_____

Important points: _____
_____
_____

Connections and questions: _____
_____
_____
_____

Applications: _____
_____
_____
_____

Notebook Template 4:
My New Thoughts About the Habitudes

The habitude of _____

In my own words: _____

_____

My images: _____

_____

_____

_____

Quotes: _____

_____

Notes: _____

_____

_____

What I can do differently: _____

_____

_____

_____

My short-term habitude goals: _____

_____

_____

My long-term habitude goals: _____

_____

_____

Questions that still remain: _____

_____

_____

Notebook Template 5:
What I Have Learned About the Habitudes

The habitude of _____

In my own words: _____

_____

My images: _____

_____

_____

_____

Quotes: _____

_____

Notes: _____

_____

_____

I'm excited to explore _____

_____

_____

I'm reminded of _____

_____

_____

I'm surprised about _____

_____

_____

I'm planning to _____

_____

_____

I'm still wondering _____

_____

_____

Habitudes Pre- and Postassessment

Visit **go.solution-tree.com/instruction** to download the handout *Habitudes Pre- and Postassessment Worksheet.*

Habitudes Pre- and Postassessment Worksheet

Name _____ Date _____

Teacher _____

Your success in school and in life depends on the habitudes you engage in. The following assessment asks you to think about and reflect on your own habitude development.

Read each statement, and think of a time or example when you demonstrated the habitude actions. Write a short note describing the situation and what you did.

Imagination

- Demonstrates an ability to connect the dots and see the big picture

- Uses foresight and intuitive perception as well as factual events to draw inferences

- Recognizes, supports, and/or champions progressive ideas

- Anticipates future trends or events

- Envisions and/or predicts possibilities others may not

- Dreams and/or talks about goals and the future

- Identifies the multiple components of problems and their relationships

- Utilizes logic and imaginative processes to analyze and solve problems

- Imagines new or revolutionary concepts, methods, models, designs, processes, and/or technology

Curiosity

- Demonstrates curiosity and enthusiasm for learning

- Uses inquiry as a way of knowing

- Asks questions beyond the text, assignment, or discussion

- Is actively interested in new technologies, processes, and methods

- Welcomes or seeks assignments requiring new skills and knowledge

- Encourages and promotes creativity and innovation

- Modifies existing concepts, methods, models, designs, processes, technologies, and systems

- Develops and tests new theories to explain or resolve complex issues

- Genuinely enjoys learning

page 1 of 3

Self-Awareness

- Projects authenticity, confidence, conviction, and passion
- Demonstrates initiative, self-confidence, resiliency, and a willingness to take responsibility for personal actions
- Possesses unwavering confidence and belief in personal capabilities
- Displays self-assurance
- Asserts self in personal and learning life
- Accepts personal responsibility for achieving personal and learning goals
- Acts independently to achieve objectives without supervision
- Expends the necessary time and effort to achieve goals
- Establishes and works toward ambitious and challenging goals

Perseverance

- Takes initiative and does whatever is necessary to achieve goals
- Bounces back after setbacks
- Functions effectively and achieves results even in adverse circumstances
- Admits mistakes and works to avoid repeating them
- Accepts personal responsibility for achieving personal and professional goals
- Functions effectively and achieves results even in adverse circumstances
- Acts decisively despite obstacles, resistance, or opposition
- Anticipates, identifies, and resolves problems or obstacles
- Utilizes logic and systematic processes to analyze and solve problems

Courage

- Takes risks for the sake of principles, values, or mission
- Inspires others with compelling visions
- Demonstrates an ability to make difficult decisions in a timely manner
- Gathers relevant input and develops a rationale for making decisions
- Evaluates the impact or consequences of decisions before making them
- Acts decisively despite obstacles, resistance, or opposition
- Accepts consequences of decisions

- Willingly corrects erroneous decisions when necessary

- Stands by or defends rationale for decisions when necessary

Passion

- Is excited about learning and life; gets turned on about the things he or she gets to learn each day

- Gets upset when things are thrown off track, especially when it relates to a topic or subject he or she shows deep excitement about

- Other learners comment on how excited they see the learner and how much he or she seems to *love* the subject or topic they are studying

- Expresses the instinctual need to pursue personal passion through such comments as, "I cannot imagine my life without . . ." or "I cannot imagine doing anything but . . ."

Adaptability

- Embraces and/or champions change

- Responds promptly to shifts in direction, priorities, and schedules

- Demonstrates agility in accepting new ideas, approaches, and/or methods

- Effective in juggling multiple priorities and tasks

- Modifies methods or strategies to fit changing circumstances

- Adapts personal style to work with different people

- Maintains productivity during transitions and even in the midst of chaos

- Expresses nontraditional perspectives and/or novel approaches

- Synthesizes and/or simplifies data, ideas, models, processes, or systems

- Challenges established theories, methods, and/or protocol

REFERENCES AND RESOURCES

Albert Einstein. (n.d.). *BrainyQuote*. Accessed at www.brainyquote.com/quotes /quotes/a/alberteins129815.html on November 12, 2011.

American Association of School Librarians. (2007). *Standards for the 21st century learner*. Chicago: Author. Accessed at www.ala.org/aasl/sites/ala.org .aasl/files/content/guidelinesandstandards/learningstandards/AASL _LearningStandards.pdf on November 11, 2011.

Armano, D. (2006, September 17). (Not) staying in the lines [Web log post]. Accessed at http://darmano.typepad.com/logic_emotion/2006/09/staying_in _the_.html on January 31, 2012.

Atkinson, B. (Ed.). (2002). *The essential writings of Ralph Waldo Emerson*. New York: Modern Library.

Bellanca, J., & Brandt, R. (Eds.). (2010). *21st century skills: Rethinking how students learn*. Bloomington, IN: Solution Tree Press.

Brisco, F., Arriaza, F., & Henze, R. C. (2009). *The power of talk: How words change our lives*. Thousand Oaks, CA: Corwin Press.

Buzan, T. (2010). *The mind map book: Unlock your creativity, boost your memory, change your life*. Upper Saddle River, NJ: Pearson Education.

CTB/McGraw-Hill. (2008). *21st century approach: Preparing students for the global workplace*. Accessed at www.ctb.com/ctb.com/control /researchArticleMainAction?p=ctbResearch&articleId=469 on November 21, 2011.

Cohen, J., Cardillo, R., & Pickeral, T. (2011). Creating a climate of respect. *Educational Leadership*, *69*(1). Accessed at www.ascd.org/publications /educational-leadership/sept11/vol69/num01/Creating-a-Climate-of -Respect.aspx on November 1, 2011.

Collins, J. (2001). *Good to great: Why some companies make the leap . . . and others don't*. New York: HarperCollins.

Creating Minds. (2010). *Scamper*. Accessed at http://creatingminds.org/tools /scamper.htm on November 15, 2011.

Csikszentmihalyi, M. (2002). *Flow: The classic work on how to achieve happiness.* New York: Harper & Row.

Curtis, J. L. (2000). *Where do balloons go?* New York: HarperCollins.

Denton, P. (2007). *The power of our words: Teacher language that helps students learn.* Turner Falls, MA: Northeast Foundation for Children.

dePaola, T. (2006). *Now one foot, now the other.* New York: Puffin.

Dr. Seuss. (1937). *And to think that I saw it on Mulberry Street.* New York: Random House.

Dorfman, C. (2003). *I knew you could.* New York: Grosset & Dunlap.

Eberle, B. (1997). *Scamper: Creative games and activities for imagination development.* Austin, TX: Prufrock.

Farrell, T. S. C. (2009). *Talking, listening, and teaching: A guide to classroom communication.* Thousand Oaks, CA: Corwin Press.

Gelb, M. J. (2003). *Discover your genius: How to think like history's ten most revolutionary minds.* New York: Harper.

Gelb, M. J., & Caldicott, S. M. (2007). *Innovate like Edison: The five-step system for breakthrough business success.* New York: Dutton.

Godin, S. (2010). *Linchpin: Are you indispensable?* New York: Portfolio.

Heaney, S. (1995). *The redress of poetry.* London: Faber.

Heard, G. (1998). *Awakening the heart: Exploring poetry in elementary and middle school.* Portsmouth, NH: Heinemann.

International Society for Technology in Education. (2007). *National technology educational standards for students* (2nd ed.). Eugene, OR: Author.

Johnston, P. H. (2004). *Choice words: How our language affects children's learning.* Portland, ME: Stenhouse.

Jukes, I., McCain, T., & Crockett, L. (2010). *Understanding the digital generation: Teaching and learning in the new digital landscape.* Kelowna, BC: 21st Century Project.

Maiers, A. (2008). *Classroom habitudes.* Clive, IA: Angela Maiers Educational Services.

Marzano, R. J., Pickering, D. J., & Pollock, J. E. (2001). *Classroom instruction that works: Research-based strategies for increasing student achievement.* Alexandria, VA: Association for Supervision and Curriculum Development.

McKenzie, J. (2005). *Learning to questions to wonder to learn.* Bellingham, WA: FNO Press.

Merriam, E. (1999). *The wise woman and her secrets.* New York: Aladdin.

Michael Jordan. (n.d.). *QuoteDB*. Accessed at www.quotedb.com/quotes/2194 on November 12, 2011.

Nielsen, L. (2010, December 26). When passion drives instruction no child is left behind [Web log post]. *The Innovative Educator.* Accessed at http://theinnovativeeducator.blogspot.com/2010/12/when-passion-drives-instruction-no.html on November 10, 2011.

Nielsen, L. (2011, January 2). Profile of a passion-driven student [Web log post]. Accessed at http://theinnovativeeducator.blogspot.com/2011/01/profile-of-passion-driven-student.html on November 10, 2011.

North Central Regional Educational Laboratory & the Metiri Group. (2003). *enGauge 21st century skills: Literacy in the digital age*. Chicago: North Central Regional Educational Laboratory.

Partnership for 21st Century Skills. (2003). *Learning for the 21st century*. Tucson, AZ: Author.

passion. (2012). In *Merriam-Webster's online dictionary*. Accessed at www.merriam-webster.com/dictionary/passion on February 6, 2012.

Paulsen, G. (2007). *Hatchet*. New York: Simon & Schuster.

Piper, W. (2005). *The little engine that could*. New York: Philomel Books.

Prensky, M. (2006). *"Don't bother me Mom—I'm learning!"* St. Paul, MN: Paragon House.

Rivero, V. (2010, September 22). 21 definitions for a 21st-century education [Web log post]. Accessed at http://edtechdigest.wordpress.com/2010/09/22/21-definitions-for-a-21st-century-education/ on November 21, 2011.

Robinson, K. (2009). *The element: How finding your passion changes everything*. New York: Penguin/Viking.

Robinson, K. (2010, May 24). *Bring on the learning revolution* [Video file]. TED Talk. Accessed at www.ted.com/talks/lang/en/sir_ken_robinson_bring_on_the_revolution.html on November 15, 2011.

Rorty, R. (2000). Being that can be understood is language. *The London Review of Books*, *22*(6), 23–25.

Small, G., & Vorgan, G. (2008). *iBrain: Surviving the technological alternation of the modern mind*. New York: HarperCollins.

Spencer, M. M. (2002, July). *What more needs saying about imagination?* Address at the 19th International Reading Association World Congress on Reading, Edinburgh, Scotland.

Sternberg, R. J. (1988). *The triangle of love: Intimacy, passion, commitment*. New York: Basic Books.

Tapscott, D. (1998). *Growing up digital: The rise of the net generation*. New York: McGraw-Hill.

Thomas Edison. (n.d.). *The phrase finder*. Accessed at www.phrases.org.uk /meanings/genius-is-one-percent-perspiration-ninety-nine-percent -perspiration.html on November 12, 2011.

Tovani, C. (2000). *I read it, but I don't get it: Comprehension strategies for adolescent readers*. Portland, ME: Stenhouse.

Tovani, C. (2004). *Do I really have to teach reading? Content comprehension, grades 6–12*. Portland, ME: Stenhouse.

21st Century Learning. (2008). *21st century learning* [Homepage]. Accessed at http://21-learn.com/ on November 21, 2011.

INDEX

Bringing Innovation to School
Suzie Boss

Activate your students' creativity and problem-solving potential with breakthrough learning projects. Across all grades and content areas, student-driven, collaborative projects will teach students how to generate innovative ideas and then put them into action.

BKF546

The Connected Educator
Sheryl Nussbaum-Beach and Lani Ritter Hall

Create a connected learning community through social media and rediscover the power of being a learner first. The authors show you how to take advantage of technology to collaborate with other educators and deepen the learning of your students.

BKF478

Creating a Digital-Rich Classroom
Meg Ormiston

Design and deliver standards-based lessons in which technology plays an integral role. This book provides a research base and practical strategies for using web 2.0 tools to create engaging lessons that transform and enrich content.

BKF385

Teaching the iGeneration
William M. Ferriter and Adam Garry

Find the natural overlap between the work you already believe in and the digital tools that define tomorrow's learning. Each chapter introduces an enduring life skill and a digital solution to enhance traditional skill-based instructional practices. A collection of handouts and supporting materials ends each chapter.

BKF393

Solution Tree | Press

a division of
Solution Tree

Visit solution-tree.com or call 800.733.6786 to order.